THUD AND WONDER

STUMBLING TOWARD HEROISM, INTEGRITY, AND TRUTH

Buddy,

Janet tells me you are
a prodigious reader.
Not bad for an elf
Hope you enjoy it.

BRIAN WEBER

082418

Publisher: Pilotage Publishing

Contact the author at www.TrueManship.com

Trademarks. This book makes descriptive references to trademarks that may be owned by others. Use of a trademarked term is not an assertion of ownership of such trademarks by the author or publisher. The mention of such trademarks is not intended to imply the existence of an association between the author or publisher and the lawful owners of such trademarks.

Scripture passages are taken from the Revised Standard Version—Second Catholic Edition (Ignatius Edition) Copyright©2006 National Council of the Churches of Christ in the United States of America. Used by permission. All rights reserved.

The stories in this book are true. Names have been changed to protect the privacy of the characters involved. All characters and incidents are real. Where the author could not recall the exact words of a conversation, the essence of the dialogue he relates is accurate, and reflects the spirit of the interaction, to the best of his memory.

Cover Illustration by Travis Schluter
Interior Illustration by Leighton Drake
Author Photo by Richard Weber

ISBN-13: 978-1-949070-00-2 (eBook)
ISBN-13: 978-1-949070-01-9 (softcover)

For Mom
Thank you for the gift of faith,
and the inspiring way you have lived it.
Your life is as Dad's was,
a life well lived, a joy forever.
Long live Iron Man.

If we insist upon being as sure as is conceivable
in every step of our course, we must be content to
creep along the ground, and can never soar.

—John Henry Cardinal Newman

CONTENTS

FOREWORD

When I met Brian, it was like a reunion with an old pal. His background was as diverse as mine. We quickly found our experiences, interests, and passions intersected in several areas.

We both have taken unusual career paths. We are risk takers and rule breakers when it comes to business as usual. Out of school, I led backcountry hiking, climbing, and canoe trips. In my early 50's my wife, Elaine, and I left our corporate jobs for a sailing adventure punctuated with extended times living and working with tourism workers in the third world.

Brian followed a similar unconventional road. After attending the Air Force Academy and active duty during the Cold War, Brian left the security of a military career to try his hand at small business entrepreneurship. He is now a freelance writer and leads men on annual excursions into nature. We both have a zeal for helping people recognize God's plan for their lives and enjoy helping others find that purpose.

Brian had been writing undercover for several years, but was waiting for what he called the "perfect situation" to officially launch his writing career. From my experience writing *Gilligan Meets Google*, I learned that ideal conditions exist only in theory. To push a new or unconventional idea out to the market we have to work in the real world. Elaine gave him two words that pushed him out of the foxhole and onto the field—"good enough." A window is open only so long before it closes on a guy and his bright idea. With a quick read of Brian's writing style, you'll agree it's a refreshing departure from the usual material in the genre of men's interests. The Rube's time is upon us.

Brian is passionate about promoting "True Manship," and his spokesman, the Rube, has a provocative and amusing voice. While Brian's writing style is easygoing, the Rube is an agitator. There aren't many authors taking on serious topics with humor and an eye for the offbeat. This is the field where Brian and the Rube stand shoulder to shoulder in the breach—wherever there's a weighty matter, a question for the ages, and no one is taking it lightly.

Dr. Charles Sanger, Writing Coach
Pilotage Group, Inc. Denton, Texas
www.CharlesSanger.com

ACKNOWLEDGMENTS

Thanks to the brave souls who subjected themselves to the torment of a Boys' Trip. You guys risked life, limb, reputation, and personal dignity. Your reward will be in the next life.

Thanks to all who encouraged me to keep writing, or lovingly poked me about why it takes so long. Thanks for the confidence you placed in my abilities.

To anyone who doubted that this project would find its way from the *Land of the Lost*, thank you for motivating me to finish something above my pay grade.

To the Friday morning Men's Study Group and the Breakfast Rat Patrol, thanks for getting me out of the cave every week.

Thanks to Charles and Elaine for your guidance, support, and motivation. And a special thank you to Garrett for introducing us.

Awesome work on the cover illustration, Travis. Well done. Thanks to Leighton for the author caricature, and Rich for the author photo. You guys had some rough raw material to work with.

Thanks to the entire family—especially Nick, Megan, Molly, Michael, Emily, and Graham—for listening to this stuff over the years, and then lying about how good it was.

A special heartfelt thanks to Vickie for her enduring hope through years of broken promises and missed deadlines. For patience and virtue uncommon in a person not yet a saint. I hope this work is something that pleases you.

And mostly, praise and thanks to God for everything that is good, true, and beautiful. I hope it pleases Him too.

SPINNING WHEEL

There are many new ideas floating around about what it means to be a man these days. The primary result of this revisionist thinking is a whole lot of confusion. This is first of all a book about manhood and manly issues, so we need to get a few things straight up front.

Western culture and mass media propose some particular examples of what a new man should look like, how he should act, and even what he should think. If you're a typical guy of the baby boomer generation, born between 1946 and 1964, it may feel like you're living on a different planet. My, how things have changed.

But there's no need to fear. After decades of shrewd, cultural observation, the Rube has come up with his own theory about men. I think men are like hamsters.

One of the biggest days in a boy's life is when he gets his first pet. Not a family pet, but one he is totally in charge of, one that is all his. I was about six when I got my first pets, a pair of hamsters. With a big assist from Mom, I furnished their cage with all the comforts of home: food, water, a nice bed of soft, aromatic litter, and a nifty exercise wheel. I gave them a killer view from a shelf high above the desk in the bedroom I shared with my older brother, Weebs. If these rats didn't have it good enough already, every night I would slip a baby spoon of ice cream between the bars. Yep, it was good to be a hamster in our house.

Though offspring of the same ham, these rats were hardly kissing cousins. Herman was large and laid back. Bigelow was small and ambitious. Each day Bigelow worked out tirelessly on the spinning wheel, while Herman ate and slept and pooped.

Every few days, housekeeping would arrive to tidy up around the cage. The Big Hand would open the cage door, wake Herman from his slumber, pluck Bigelow from the wheel, and set them both outside the cage in the free world that was our tiny suburban house on Normandy Road. Herman would stay in the bedroom not far from the cage, while Bigelow scurried all over the house in search of adventure. When it was time to go back in the cage, Herman would be trembling at the cage door, but Bigelow would be the subject of an all-out ham hunt. He could be anywhere in the house.

Having once tasted freedom, Bigelow was a rat with a new mission in life. I came home from school each afternoon to discover him hammering away on the cage door with his little buckteeth. Every so often he would stop and test the door with his nose. Nope. Back to work. When he wasn't pounding away, he was working out. One way or another, his wheels were always turning.

One fateful day, Bigelow hammers on the door just right, and the locking pin pops out of its hasp. He tests the door, and voila! A free rat. Oh, the adventures Bigelow would have driving the jeep for the Rat Patrol all day. Meanwhile Herman slept his life away in ease and comfort.

Freedom is good, but fraught with peril. A free-range rat can get into a lot of trouble. The Big Hand knows what's best for Bigelow. He needs protection from the hazards of the outside world, so that night the Big Hand picks up the hamster cage and turns it around. From then on Bigelow would go to the same side of the cage and hammer away where the cage door used to be. His hamster brain couldn't comprehend that the door was now on the other side. Bigelow's ticket to freedom was forever out of his reach. Herman, having experienced neither elation nor disappointment, just yawned and snoozed.

Most men are a lot like either Herman or Bigelow. We spend the first half of our lives working to achieve security and comfort. Once we've earned a life relatively free from pain and turmoil, some of us turn inward. We forfeit any dreams of greatness we may have had when we were young. In essence, our lives become an exercise of running out the clock while avoiding hardship and struggle. These are the Hermans of the world.

Other men sense an emptiness, a feeling that something is missing in their safe world, so they spend the rest of their lives trying to escape from it. These are the Bigelows.

The Big Hand knows Bigelow will never be content, so it does its utmost to keep him occupied. There are lots of toys to fill a restless rat's waking hours, and everyone has something new to sell him. The culture has a vested interest in keeping him in the cage. It must fool the ambitious hamster into thinking that it's pointless to search for the cage door. There is no escape. Be happy in the cage. He mustn't know that true freedom exists.

When we are kids, our universe is constantly expanding. Our world grows from our house to our street, to our neighborhood, to our subdivision. And each expansion brings new and wondrous experiences. As grown men we seek the same sense of awe, wonder, and excitement we felt as kids, but it is strangely missing. We turn to all sorts of things hoping to fill the void—money, possessions, pleasures, thrills, sex, status, recognition, and achievement. The moment we get too close to true freedom, the Big Hand is there to turn our world around with the latest revolutionary thing we can't live without. And Bigelow, unable to determine true north, gets back on the wheel again.

Some guys spend their entire lives running the rat race ever faster, so busy they don't think about the void. Their snazzy hamster hotels are indeed bigger with the latest rope swings and activity assault courses, but they're still cages, and in the end the stuff is still just litter.

Thankfully, there is an alternative to the Big Hand. The Rube is no pop culture guru, but he stumbled on an acorn by accident many years ago, and has been gnawing on it ever since.

Out of this nut was hatched the idea of a Boy's Trip, an annual adventure where, for a brief time, the Rube and a few of his pals leave behind comfort, convenience, and routine. We go to places in nature where not everything is safe, where busyness gives way to mystery and surprise, where we escape the sway of the culture's Big Hand.

But you mustn't think this is all just fun and games. We also have an important mission, should we decide to accept it—to uncover the essential questions. Things buried deeper every day under the perpetual noise and distractions of a corrosive culture.

The Rube is a thoroughly amateur guide, so every Boy's Trip is bound to have a few rough patches. But a little hardship is a good builder of character. Though we may start the trip as tired, timid hamsters, we return with renewed vigor and vitality. We rejoin the battle a mite more like the noble, caped rodent, Mighty Mouse, with a keener vision, and more courageous, more willing, and better able to save the day.

DAMN THE TORPEDOES

The Boys' Trip was not originally my idea. An annual getaway strictly for guys is hardly a unique concept. The classic buddy trip has been around a long time, but the first one I remember is *City Slickers* in the early nineties. Let's be honest. Good-time escapism is the primary goal of such a trip, at least initially. Anything else is strictly a byproduct. A guy doesn't sign up for one of these looking for deep reflection and contemplation. Pondering is not the objective. Those trips are called retreats. The Boys' Trip is no retreat.

The inspiration for the first junket came from a pal who was moving from Phoenix to Montana. He was looking for a way to stay connected with a couple of his desert rat buddies. It was Glenn's idea to fly Pierce and me to Big Sky Country for a long weekend. It's possible Glenn wanted to show off his two mountain properties with their new custom cabins. But not likely. Glenn, aka the Hobbit, is different from the typical guy in many ways, and not just because of his stature and his hairy feet.

I first met Glenn when I rode with him from Phoenix to Agua Prieta, Mexico for a parish mission trip. A group of men was traveling down to do construction work at an orphanage.

Glenn's job was to do something constructive, while I was there to provide grunt labor and comic relief. We all have our gifts. I'm inepter than Tim "The Tool Man" Taylor on a job site, so Glenn was tasked with accident prevention and, failing that, damage control. From that point, I think he took the Rube on as a reclamation project. A generous soul, the Hobbit is always doing stuff like that.

So, the first Boys' Trip was the Hobbit's doing.

It was early October 2001 and only a few weeks after the terror attacks of 9/11. In those harrowing days, air travel was in a state of upheaval. Months before, Glenn had purchased tickets for us to fly from Phoenix to Great Falls, and it would be understandable if he decided to cancel the trip under the circumstances. But Glenn is not just a good friend, he's a patriotic American. Coincidentally, he bears an uncanny resemblance to Rudy Giuliani, the mayor of New York City when 9/11 occurred.

According to Mayor Hobbit, it's our duty to show the bad guys that terrorism isn't going to cause America, the home of the brave, to become a land of fraidy-cats. The 2001 World Series would not be canceled; it went on to become historic, and so would we. We'd do this trip for the healing of the nation. Damn the torpedoes, full speed ahead.

On the surface, the Boys' Trip doesn't appear much different from the golfing, fishing, or gambling trips that old teammates, classmates, or fraternity brothers do together. These are opportunities to rehash tales of past glory and to renew old friendships. Most guys have very few close friends, so becoming a true friend is a noble enough cause. But is it possible that the Boys' Trip could actually serve an even higher purpose?

Every good Boys' Trip begins and ends in the wild. We go outside our safe surroundings to an environment slightly discomfiting. In nature we're not in control, and things profound and unpredictable await. Creation provides clues to some of life's deepest mysteries, and if a guy is seriously searching for answers, he seeks to get close to the source.

Honestly, at first, we didn't intentionally save space or make room or time for anything or anyone else besides us three amigos. Our goal was to get away from the artificial world for a time. To clear the decks and open up hearts and minds to fresh inputs.

You've probably heard the platitude about God meeting you wherever you are. I wouldn't be so sure about that. If you were God, where would you want to hang out? Most likely it would be where you don't have to compete with a bazillion sources of man-made noise, temptations, and distractions.

From the first Boys' Trip, with even the briefest introspection, came the inescapable sensation that something or someone else was at work here. At the very least, looking on with bewilderment or amusement.

After our initial foray to Montana, Glenn, Pierce, and I made an informal covenant to make the Boys' Trip an annual deal. When we toasted our fellowship with Moose Drool, a tradition was born.

These stories are taken from events that actually happened. In good conscience, a guy can't just make this stuff up. Only the names have been changed to protect the guilty. We're all way past the age of innocence.

THE SNEFFELS SANCTION

G reat mountains, like great stories, capture man's imagination. High peaks draw men like magnets draw
iron. The gold standard for hikers and climbers in
America is the 14er, a mountain over 14,000 feet high. Peak
baggers worldwide stalk the 14er in pursuit of many things.
Some look for adventure; others seek inspiration; and some
seek to prove their manhood. Whatever the reason, it's all the
stuff of legends.

Colorado, which boasts fifty-three 14ers, is the destination
for this year's Boys' Trip. The Rube is no peak bagger, but it's
time the boys and I push the proverbial envelope and set our
sights a bit higher. We're going to bag us a 14er.

Base camp will be a pair of rustic cabins in Ouray, a
charming hamlet in southwest Colorado. Nestled in a valley
surrounded by awe-inspiring peaks, Ouray calls itself the
Switzerland of America. Here, I have my pick of a half-dozen
14ers, and the Rube settles on a mountain they call Sneffels.
Seriously, Rube?

I know what you're thinking. The setting for a heroic
mountain adventure should be a legendary peak, like say, the
Matterhorn or the Eiger. Nobody will be impressed to hear

that we conquered Sneffels. What exactly did that noble feat require? An entire case of tissues? Beating Sneezy and the other Six Dwarfs to the summit? Whistling while we hike? Very funny, wise guy. Hear me out.

The name Sneffels may not strike fear in a man's heart, but it's enough to make him rummage through his fanny pack for a hankie. A telltale sniffle can be quite fearsome to a manly man who's not supposed to let anyone see him cry. Tears? What tears? "It's my allergies." That kind of guy. Besides, we're not doing this to impress anybody. Right?

I figured we'd beat the season's first snow in the San Juan Mountains, but an early cold blast dumped fourteen inches the day before. The pristine powder is a glorious backdrop for the deep evergreens and the blazing yellow aspens, but not all is picture perfect. I do wonder, could this be a higher power throwing a wet blanket on my peak-bagging plans?

After a nine-hour drive from Arizona, we arrive at Ouray's Riverside Inn and Cabins way after dark. One of the boys, Rollie, has one look at the Rube's rustic camping cabins and takes a cozy room in the lodge. The other guys follow suit. I'm afraid I have a bunch of prima donnas on my hands. Since when do mountain men need toilets, running water, and Egyptian cotton sheets? What's next, boys? Lavender body wash and scented loofahs? I better settle a few things with these guys right now. After I collect those little chocolates off their pillows.

In the morning, I impress on the guys that Saturday's big hike will be no tiptoe through the tulips. We won't pack a picnic basket or a quilted blanket. I warn them, don't be looking for a nanny and her flock of adorable children. Sneffels is no place for pirouettes and holding hands. And I don't want to see any lederhosen outside this room. You say the novice nun was in Austria, not Switzerland? Close enough. Anyhow, I'm done babying these guys. From here on, they had better be ready for sweating and straining and grunting. Powering our way over rugged terrain. Man stuff. No, sir. Sneffels will be no picnic.

The reputation of the 14er is somewhat intimidating. I've done a 14er before, so I can talk the talk. My trophy was Pike's Peak in Colorado Springs. That was many years ago, and as I recall there's a paved road all the way up. I drove to the top, got out of the car, and walked across the parking lot to the summit. It was brutal. My right butt cheek was numb for half the drive. So, I don't know if any of us has the right stuff for a real 14er, least of all me. We might be just a bunch of soft city boys; the kind real mountain men call flatlanders.

The big hike is only one part of a well-rounded Boys' Trip. Our first day is a rafting excursion through the Black Canyon of the Gunnison River. We've got to rise early to meet our river guides at their shop in Ridgway. The sun is barely up when the Rube and his cohort of five sleepy dwarfs arrive and pile into the shop's van for the two-hour drive northeast to the river.

I'm sitting in the first row of seats, and the river guides are up front. We've been on the road a half-hour when I get shotgun's attention by tapping him on the shoulder. "Hey, Baxter, we're planning to hike Mt. Sneffels tomorrow. Which one of these hills is Sneffels?"

He peers out the passenger window, wipes the glass with his sleeve, and says with a grimace, "That's her at four o'clock, sticking up above all the snow."

Even through the haze of a grimy van window, Mt. Sneffels, with its radical, vertical relief of over 7,000 feet is breathtaking.

"That's way up there." I gulp.

Baxter gives me a wry grin and shakes his head. "Sneffels ain't for hiking anymore this year, dude. She's just for lookin' now. Better come up with another plan." From the looks of the greenhorns in back, he must be thinking we flatlanders have as good a chance of climbing Sneffels as he has of walking on the Gunnison River.

I lean forward and press Baxter further, "Have you ever done Sneffels?"

He shakes his head, "Naw. But I've heard some stories. She's tough enough on the best of days, dude. Under snow and ice, you don't want any part of her."

That last comment settles it for me. If I let the niggling doubts of a hayseed paddle foot paralyze us, we'll spend the whole weekend watching football on the lodge sofa. My spine stiffening, I decide I'm going for the Big Snuffy, snow or no snow. And I'm taking these guys with me. If there are any tales to tell, we're gonna be the ones telling them. I settle back in my seat, defiant on the outside, a tad uneasy on the inside.

Today is the last day of the rafting season, and the Gunnison is more a float than a whitewater ride. The rafting is too mellow for my liking, but there's some excitement when Pierce bounces out of the raft on the first rapid. Though I wasn't looking for relaxation, an easy ride is the best thing for us today. These guys will be well rested for the big hike tomorrow.

Colorado weather is notorious for afternoon thunderstorms, so every guidebook warns hikers to be off any peak by noon. If you're going for a 14er, you best get an early start—the darker the better. My motivational skills are not what they once were because the Rube and his cohorts are not up and out until 10:00 a.m. Not even my pathetic warbling of "Edelweiss" is enough to get them out from under the covers. The boys still think this is some kind of vacation.

As we're gathering our gear, the group is strangely quiet. I get the distinct feeling that these guys are not fired up about hiking Sneffelpuss or Snuffelupagus or whatever. Hiking a 14er, especially one under snow and ice, is a daunting proposition. None of us wants to be the first to admit it. As you know, guys are not good at sharing: beers, fries, or feelings.

The trailhead for Sneffels is at Yankee Boy Basin, and it's nine miles from Ouray on a dirt road. Two days of snowmelt has turned the road into a muddy mess. After forty minutes of sloppy sledding, we're into the foothills, where the road has vanished under virgin snow. There's no sign of a trailhead, and the needling from the skeptics in my truck is starting to get under my skin. Judging by the radio chatter, the skeptics in truck number two are thinking that the rafting guide, Baxter, was right. There's nobody out here. A few beers and a soak in the famous Ouray hot springs sounds like a better plan.

We did pass one other human a couple miles back. The guy had parked his Subaru and was running on the shoulder up the road. He was a thin, middle-aged man wearing only light running shoes, shorts, and a lightweight shirt. He could have been jogging in Phoenix. We are way better prepared than that guy, I thought. He's not going far dressed like that. He's probably looking for a field of daisies and a soft spot to spread out his blanket.

Thinking that now is as good a time as any to face the music, I tell Max to stop the truck and let Rollie's group pull up alongside us. After some spirited negotiation, er, discussion, we agree to button up the trucks right here and have a go at it. It's blustery but not too cold; the temperature is in the low forties. It's a nice day to play in the snow if nothing else. We can't do that in the desert.

By the time we're all geared up, we look like a pack of Himalayan Sherpas. After tying my shoes one last time, I'm surprised to find an extra head in the huddle. It's the man we saw running back there on the shoulder. "I'm here to hike Sneffels," he says, "but I don't want to go solo. Can I go with you guys?"

Sizing him up, I ask, "Have you been up there before?"

He looks down at the device in his palm. "No, but I've got a GPS, and I can track it."

This is back in the day when only serious hikers have GPS units, so I'm thinking this Running Man could be a real godsend. I just hope he doesn't slow us down. I have no idea how ludicrous that thought would turn out to be. I turn back to the visitor and say, "Sure, you can come."

Running Man doesn't look like the type of guy who will sit still for the Rube's official safety briefing, so I have to hope he has everything he needs. The last thing we semi-professional adventurers want is some tenderfoot geezer holding us back because he doesn't have the right gear. His only equipment is a minimal hydration pack. On the plus side, he's so lean he can't weigh much more than my daypack. Even weaklings like us can carry him out if we have to. If we take turns.

Running Man has his own idea of what hiking solo is because he takes off like a snow hare and is out of sight in mere minutes. Fortunately for us, he leaves a set of footprints in the deep snow, the only evidence suggesting he is more than a phantom.

It's 11:15 a.m. when we lumber off in a line following Running Man's tracks. We're starting at around 11,500 feet in elevation, so it's no surprise that the beefier boys, Rollie and Max, are laboring in the altitude from the get go. The snowdrifts are two to three feet deep in spots, but the footing is firm, so we make steady progress. The sky is a kaleidoscope of fast-moving clouds decorating the mountains with a rippling curtain of fascinating shadows. This is heavenly.

One of the Rube's rules for a flagship hike is to agree in advance on certain bailout points along the route. That way, a group of guys of different abilities and fitness levels can make their goal, and others can go further if they're able. For this trek, Blue Lakes Pass is the first bailout point at two miles and 13,000 feet.

We reach the pass at around 12:45 p.m., and Rollie and Max are really breathing hard. Neither is blue yet, but it's clear they've had enough. They should be pleased. Blue Lakes Pass is a worthy destination, especially on a day like today. This place is so beautiful it's almost hypnotic. It's tempting to stay here. Max is a Boy Scout troop leader so he can pitch tents for Moses and Elijah and the Rube. These other boys will expect a cushy loft with a view. I think we've got one of those. Lord, it is good that we are here.

After a ten-minute break, Rollie and Max head back down to the trucks. The weather is holding so far, so the rest of us decide to see what's up around the bend. Curiously, the deep snow seems to have skipped over the mountain up here. Instead, we're faced with a forbidding jumble of huge boulders and spires. Above the pass, the granite slabs are so steep the first snow of the season slides right off. From below, the profile of this gnarly ridge resembles a rusty limb saw with a long row of teeth jutting skyward, all twisted and bent. There's not even a hint of a trail.

We've covered only 150 feet when we're pinched single-file onto a dead-end ledge not more than two feet wide. Below us is a sheer drop of at least forty feet. Above us is a steep rock face of nine or ten feet. If a guy was looking for a convenient off-ramp, he just found it.

Pierce is quick to hit the eject button. "I don't need this," he sputters. He turns toward his brother.

"I'm with you, bro," Kurt nods. "Blue Lakes Pass is awesome, this here, not so much."

A guy doesn't like to give up too soon, but this is a good call by the brothers. Pierce has never been a fan of heights. Pierce and Kurt maneuver around Van and me, and we watch them disappear around the bend.

Alone now, Van and I are teetering in limbo between courage and timidity. Or is it between bravado and sensibility? This is our last chance to bail. We're on our third round of paper-rock-scissors when Running Man appears on the pitched rock, ten feet over our heads. He assures us, "Guys, I know the way from here. Just follow me, and you'll be fine."

Before I can spit a word out, he's gone again. I have a growing uneasiness. We can't just leave Running Man alone up here, can we? If he wanted to leave us behind, he could have easily done it. But he came back for us, so he's become attached to us for some strange reason. Loosely attached, but connected nevertheless. Van and I agree to soldier on. Leave no man behind. Or ahead, in this case.

Climbing Sneffels via this route is a class 3 scramble a mile long with more than 1,100 feet of gain and, ahem, some exposure. We're not talking about sunburn. There's also the risk of becoming stranded or dead-ended. Worst case, then, it's dying by blunt trauma, freezing to death, or starvation. But I've always been an optimist.

My feet are stuck to the rock as I watch Van begin climbing after Running Man. Somebody has to go first. Somebody with courage. I take a deep breath and scramble up the nine-foot rock face behind him. On top of the rock, I'm thinking, *I sure hope we can keep going forward from here, because there's no way I'm going back down this way.* Is this the proverbial point of no return?

Our every move must be careful and deliberate. The tension is relentless, and the going is excruciatingly slow. Van climbs faster than me, so although we're in this mess together, it's like we're climbing alone. This is not a social event.

There's no denying the sense of satisfaction in getting over or around each obstacle, and it does increase a guy's confidence for the next one. But by the time we get to number fifty and there's no end in sight, I wonder if the odds are starting to work against us. The undercurrent of anxiety is bubbling to the surface. The idea of trying to return this same route in waning daylight—or worse, in a thunderstorm—is too much to think about right now. How can it be that a place so utterly glorious feels so strangely godforsaken?

About ninety minutes into this ordeal, the ominous dark clouds are building and Running Man is nowhere to be found. Big surprise. About two and a half hours in and my mind drifts to a dreamlike state. I wish this were just a dream. I would be so relieved and so happy to have my boring, regular life back. Alas, when I return from Disney's *Fantasia*, I'm still between the same rock and a hard place. Except for the wind, it's eerily quiet up here. There is much silence but no peace.

About sixty vertical feet separate us, with me trailing, when Van hits the wall. He plops down on a thin shelf and uncorks a scorching barrage the likes of which I haven't heard before or since. The scrubbed version includes the phrases, "the dumbest thing I have ever done in my entire life," and, "the biggest idiot on the face of the earth." The gravity of our predicament hits me as hard as that 1958 Buick once did. That idiot is you, Rube. I'm responsible for getting Van into this pickle, and I need help if we're going to get out of the brine.

At any other time, the moment I sit down to pray, my mind starts careening out of control, flitting from one random thought to another. I've heard that imminent danger has a way of bringing the mind into clear focus. I don't know if that's true, but for the first time in my life, I pray like my life depends on it. It's a concentrated, undiluted, full-strength supplication. I'm sure the fervent prayer of the saints is like music to God, but this stuff coming from me sounds suspiciously like pitiful begging. I don't recall praying anything like, "I'm turning it over to you, God," or, "Jesus, take the wheel," but maybe in my pathetic wailing that's what He heard.

I'm about to scratch my prayer on an envelope and stuff it in a crack in the rock when words from a faint voice float by on the wind. I leap to my feet. It's the still, small voice! It's real! Followed by an agonizing silence. And then doubt. Am I losing my mind?

Then I hear the call distinctly. "Hello! Are you guys out there? Are you OK?" It's not the voice of God; it's Running Man. But at this point, I'll take it.

From about 120 feet above Van, he calls again. "Keep climbing, guys. I'm on the roof! You've almost got it!"

The crux just below the summit is the most technically difficult pitch of the day, but with our mental burdens lifted,

Van and I scale the steep notch like we're as light as feathers. In mere minutes, we're standing triumphant on the summit of Mt. Sneffels, 14,150 feet above sea level. For the serious peak bagger, the summit experience can be overrated. I must not be anywhere near ready for the big time, because I'm higher than a kite right now.

I drop my backpack next to the thick PVC tube containing the summit register. It's party time. I scour my gear for the two beers I'm sure Running Man stashed in my pack back at the huddle. Drat. Of course, the legendary libations are figments of my monkey brain imagination. That kind of stuff only happens in the movies. I'll have to settle for my camera and the radio.

I'm ready to share my joy with the boys down below. My cheap radio battery has enough juice left to get one call out. I'm ecstatic, "Guys we made it! We're on the summit!"

Rollie answers, loaded for bear. "You idiot!" he barks. "Do you know what time it is? It's after three, and this storm is moving in. You guys could die up there!"

My brief visit to cloud nine ends with an unceremonious thud. Rollie is right, of course. I deserve a good scolding. I have no right to expect praise or encouragement. Any reasonable hiker would have been down three hours ago. Running Man would be half-way home by now if not for us. If we actually get back alive, I don't expect the boys to pick us up, or to retrieve the bodies if we don't. Rollie is really mad. I swallow hard, at a loss for words. But I don't need any words at the moment. The meek squeak in my hand is the dying gasp of the radio's battery. We are officially out of touch.

I need to get some pictures while we have Running Man captive. He snaps a photo of Van and me with the Telluride ski mountain two thousand snowy feet below us. I take one of Running Man just to see if he will show up on film. I pull the summit register from the tube and jot a short note of praise and thanksgiving. At least the written record will attest to whom full credit is due. Running Man gets the assist.

The brief moment of triumph is my chance to find out what makes this guy go. Faking nonchalance like I just bumped into him at Denny's, I prod, "So, tell me, what's a guy like you doing in a place like this?" *Very smooth, Rube.*

He says he's retired and climbing tall mountains is his hobby. Other guys collect shells, coins, or cars. Running Man is a peak bagger. I can't believe my good fortune. Just to survive this ordeal to the summit is enough, but now I have a chance to study the elusive, secretive creature up close. I learn that he's a sixty-two-year-old retired engineer. Being a relatively young buck of fifty-something, sixty-two sounds ancient to me. I'm thinking, *How does an old guy get to be in this kind of shape?*

"Just curious, do you always hike like you're escaping a fire?"

Running Man says he used to be faster before suffering a fall in Yosemite. He adds, "I'm more careful now. I'm taking it slow today." He's serious. I don't think he knows how to joke.

I deadpan, "Yeah, we've been quite worried about you. We thought we might have to carry you out of here. How bad was the fall?"

Multiple fractures, he admits. He was transported by airlift to a hospital. Looks like he made a full recovery.

Every question to Running Man feels like an interrogation. He's not hostile, but he's not exactly Mister Glib either. That's about all we're going to get out of him. Running Man is fidgeting like a kid who has to pee. It's after 3:30 p.m., and no hiker in his right mind is on a peak at this hour. And whatever else he may be, Running Man is not crazy.

It should be reassuring to know that this guy has experienced a life-threatening fall from a mountain. Surely, he would never hike anywhere dangerous or risky again after such a harrowing episode. Right. It didn't dawn on me until much later why he would drag a couple of novices up a serious mountain like this; we are his safety net. Maybe Running Man hasn't learned that much after all. Relying on the Rube to save him is by far the most foolish move of the day.

Leading us over to the northwest edge of the summit, Running Man says we're taking a different route down. I'm elated, but once again only momentarily. After taking one look down the chute, my knees buckle. This is not the cakewalk I was hoping for.

He glances at his GPS and points. "This way. Follow me."

But I'm not done stalling. "Wait, how far is it this way?"

Running Man has had enough of my dawdling. "About halfway," he says, straight-faced. And with that, he begins rock-hopping down the steep couloir like a spooked mountain goat. We catch one more glimpse of him ten minutes later, at the base of the gully, and after that, we never see Running Man again.

The down climb is four miles of tortured sliding down steep fields of unstable talus and slipping on muddy slopes strewn with boulders. It's a dreadful, miserable, wonderful slog. I'm worried about wrenching a knee or dislocating an ankle with the slightest misstep. But it's better than dying with the slightest misstep. On any other day, I would be cursing this hike, but not this day. I am a changed man.

After three exhausting hours, the storm clouds are still swirling about the mountain. Somehow the lightning and rain have steered clear. Van and I are limping along in near darkness at the base of the mountain when a dirt road appears beneath our battered feet. Mercy, that feels better.

A short time later, the growing rumble of an approaching vehicle is a welcome disruption of the dusky stillness. Before we can hang out a thumb, the vehicle rolls to a stop and the driver motions for us to hop in the back of the truck. I know hitchhiking is dangerous, but hey, we're on a winning streak. We haven't seen another soul besides Running Man all day, and these guys show up out of thin air. Who else can they be but angels picking up his torch? Doing one more good deed before flying away home for the night. God knows they've had a long day already, what with holding off the wind, the rain, and the fury. Just for a couple of tenderfoot greenhorns.

The free ride around the base of Sneffels saves at least an hour of gimpy wobbling on legs long gone rubbery. To our relief and surprise, the boys and their trucks are sitting in the dark at the junction with Yankee Boy Basin.

Our ride slows to a stop; we wave our thanks to the Samaritans up front, and hobble out of the truck. I join two other guys in Max's truck, but it feels like I'm alone. On the drive back to town, the mood is subdued. There seems to be little joy in Mudville.

Back in Ouray, there's only one joint open after 9:00 p.m. As luck would have it, our rafting guide, Baxter, is sitting at the bar. It's pretty dark in here, but he recognizes us straight away. A gaggle of six tourists in a small place is hard to miss.

Baxter slides off his barstool and strides over to our table with a broad smile. "What's up, boys? You guys have a good day today?"

Max pipes up first, "Yeah. We did a little hiking."

Baxter responds, "Really? Where to?"

The boys are busy settling into their chairs, so I jump in. "Sneffels. Mt. Sneffels."

He replies, "Cool. How are the fall colors? There are lots of pretty meadows in the foothills."

I reply, "We didn't see any meadows. Just snow."

He shoots back, "Sure. Up higher. How far did you guys go? Yankee Boy?" I nod. "Blue Lakes?" I nod again. He swallows, "Sneffels?"

I give him a look that says, "I told you so."

Baxter's eyes bulge like they're trying to buck his eyebrows off. "Are you kidding? To the summit?"

I boast, "Well, yeah. Like I said." As if it were ever in doubt.

"No way!" He exclaims, giving us two thumbs up. "Unbelievable! Good going, chaps!"

Baxter turns from our table with a bemused look on his weathered face. He's scratching his head as he shuffles back to the bar. As an adventure guide for landlubbers and other soft city dwellers, he probably has a lot of unlikely stories. Now he can add the tale of a group of raw flatlanders blundering up where they don't belong and stumbling their way to victory.

I'm feeling pretty full of myself. Every guy wants to be validated as more of a man in the eyes of the world. I imagine we've proven ourselves a bit more like real mountain men tonight, and that feels really good.

INTERLUDE: WHAT'S YOUR MQ?

The culture conditions guys to think of manliness as a competitive sport. And a contest is not a real sport until you keep score or keep time. A guy needs a way to measure himself against other men on the manliness scale. The Rube proposes that every guy comes equipped with an onboard mechanism to perform this function. Just for fun we'll call it his manometer.

The manometer is not like a typical fitness monitor. It doesn't measure objective values like time, distance, and elevation gain. It counts man points. Man points are earned by accomplishing specific actions and are used to compute a guy's Manliness Quotient (MQ).

It sounds scientific, but the MQ is highly subjective and situational. For example, backing up a boast is a plus one man point. Disproving a naysayer, another plus one. Weeping of any variety is a big minus.

We rationalize any action that might subtract points from our MQ. On the Sneffels affair, I'm excusing my whimpering and wailing. Technically, they're not weeping. If I'm honest, I'd be lucky to break even on the whole ordeal. It makes no sense that a guy can be less of a man after doing something like this, right? You see how this works. Men are so practiced at giving ourselves the benefit of the doubt.

At the end of the day, the boys' subdued spirits gave me a nagging sense that perhaps all was not well. In a moment of rare empathy, I put myself in their shoes. Think about it, Rube. I didn't ask the boys to sacrifice an entire afternoon and evening so I could indulge what they likely regarded a reckless pursuit. And they were selfless and generous anyway.

I never expected them to stay long after dark to shuttle us out of the wilderness, yet they patiently waited for hours anyway. I didn't ask Van's forgiveness for getting him into a jam he didn't bargain for. And he displayed brotherhood and showed me mercy anyway.

Sure, Van and I made the summit, and that may be a boost to the bogus MQ, but who displayed the greater virtue? Wasn't it the guys who exercised sound judgment and didn't willfully exceed the limits of their conditioning and abilities? In the end, isn't the measure of a man's virtue the only scale that matters?

The notches on a peak bagger's belt don't come easy. The pinnacles of earth and rock are attained only through effort and struggle. But can hardship and challenge also help us climb the spiritual peaks to new heights of heroic virtue? Endurance, perseverance, patience, gratitude, and forgiveness are the raw materials of True Manship. Can we find those on the trail?

A shot at bagging a trophy peak or some other emblem of achievement is motivating. But how often do we challenge each other to be peak baggers of a different and better kind, men who strive for the supernatural summits of the soul?

BLOWIN' IN THE WIND

The Rube is partial to adventures off the beaten path, far from the maddening crowd. He generates plenty of madness on his own.

When one of the boys suggests a rafting trip through the Grand Canyon, of course, I'm immediately skeptical. This is one of those classic trips bound to be on a few million bucket lists. Before you blow it off, think about it, Rube—a great geological wonder unfolding before us as we lounge in luxury while a professional staff tends to our every need. It does have a certain intrigue. I owe it to the boys to at least check it out.

It's no surprise when I find that all river trips in the national park are strictly regulated. A permit for a private trip typically takes several years of waiting, and that only gets you a chance in the lottery. Commercial trips are easier to obtain but require at least two weeks of vacation time and the payment of a four-digit price tag. This is not a quest one enters into frivolously.

Still, I might have been persuaded. That is, until I learn of the legendary, horrible smelly beast rumored to track every rafting group through the canyon. This thing is so relentless even the best river guides are unable to shake it. The beast has become such an integral part of the folklore of the canyon that it has earned its own nickname. Loch Ness has the fabled monster; the Grand Canyon has the Groover.

This beauty is the official portable toilet mandated by the federal government to be carried on all Grand Canyon rafting trips. All deposits in the canyon must be made in the magic crapper, or the violator is subject to federal prosecution. How the feds enforce this program must be one of the most closely held secrets in the nation. Don't ask me how, but the feds will track you down. Holy crap! Could wayward doody contain fingerprints or DNA in it? Either way, the doody of a good citizen is to obey, not to question how or why. Sorry.

Every rafting group must pack a dutifully loaded Groover out at the end of the trip. The idea of floating the Colorado River for 226 miles with fourteen days of deposits from twenty people is enough to make a guy want to hold it for two weeks. Having always been one who operates on the fringe, the Rube will find another way to float the Canyon if there's one to be found.

In the process of tidying up the man cave one early morning, I stumble on an article from an ancient travel rag describing a section of the Colorado River below Glen Canyon Dam, just east of where the national park begins. Here the river is a serene float beneath soaring cliffs with water that is blue-green, clear, and cold. The idyllic stretch runs for fifteen miles, ending at Lees Ferry, where all the canyon rafting trips begin. It's perfect. The hordes are all going in the opposite direction. The Rube will deliver the essential Colorado River experience with none of the hassles. That's what I do. The Rube's Bargain Adventures for Guys. Adventures for Less. Less time. Less money. Less crap.

It's day three of our first southern Utah trip, and Chad, Pierce, and I are coming off two days of hiking over twenty miles in the Paria River Canyon and Buckskin Gulch. The boys are ready for a relaxing float trip. A day of sitting butt side and going with the flow, letting the river do the work. That's the plan, anyway. I've reserved three kayaks from a dive shop in Page, Arizona. We'll transport them to the river at Lees Ferry, where a water taxi is waiting to run us upriver to the base of the Glen Canyon Dam.

When we arrive in Page, the shop is locked up tight. It's Saturday around 10:00 a.m. It's a strange time to be closed. I peer through the front glass door and catch a glimpse of a guy in the shop. We go around and try the back door, which is unlocked. I walk in like I own the joint. "Is Trace here?"

The guy looks up from working on a trailer hitch. "You're lookin' at him."

We're in a hurry, so the Rube dispenses with common courtesy. "You have some kayaks you're holding for us. We're ready for them."

Trace straightens up, grabbing a towel from his back pocket. He wipes his brow, and his expression is not happy. "Are you the guys from the Valley?"

I'm relieved. "Yeah. That's us."

He grimaces, shaking his head. "I have some bad news for you boys. The wind has been so bad that I cancelled all our river trips this weekend. I tried to get a hold of you guys, but your number wasn't working."

I'm broadsided by this news. "Oh, man, we've been out of cell service the past two days hiking the slots up in Utah."

Trace nods. "Yeah, I remember now. You're lucky you caught me. I wasn't coming in to the shop today. I don't know why. I just stopped in for a second. Sorry, fellas. You're out of luck. Maybe if you had a couple more days. Don't sweat it, though. I didn't charge your deposit." He turns back to his work like the conversation is over.

If Trace thinks we're just going to see ourselves out, he's in for a Rube awakening. I'm not accustomed to giving up anything without a fight.

"Trace, I don't get it. What's so bad about this weather? It seems fine to me."

He's annoyed at my challenging his judgment. "Dude, the weather's not bad at the moment. It's the forecast for today that's the problem. Winds up to forty miles an hour and maybe more rain. It's supposed to kick up in the afternoon, just like yesterday. Trust me. I know the canyon."

I've never been one to put much stock in predictions. If you recall, we were supposed to be thrown back to the Stone Age at the turn of the millennium. How did that forecast turn out?

I give him my best puppy dog sad face. "Listen, Trace, we have today, and that's it for this year's trip. We plan on this for a whole year. It's not like we can just come back tomorrow and try again." He appears to be softening.

I lean in for the close. "To the real adventurer, braving the elements is part of the deal. They don't cancel the Running of the Bulls for a little drizzle, do they? I could understand it if you were talking to a pack of Brownies." I pause for effect. "You know, Trace, your coming in to the shop today and our being here at the exact same time was not an accident. We're both meant to be here. It's destiny."

He likely hasn't heard this kind of motivational drivel since his high school football days. Trace glances at Chad and Pierce. They're supposed to be nodding like bobble heads but they're not. I'll deal with them later. To my surprise, Trace relents, but not before issuing a final warning, "Last taxi is at 11:00. If you miss it, you don't get your money back. No refunds." He probably figures I deserve what's coming to me. A hard-headed guy has to get his lessons the hard way.

By the time we get the kayaks loaded and the trailer hooked up to Chad's truck, we have thirty minutes to make the sixty-minute drive to Lees Ferry. The day's adventure begins right now. When we squeal up to the marina boat ramp it's past 11:00 a.m., but the taxi is still there, and there's a guy on board.

I holler from the top of the boat ramp, "Man, are we happy to see you!"

He smiles and waves. "Come on down!". Our taxi driver is downright congenial. "Truth is, I'm happier to see you guys than you are to see me. You're my only fare for the whole weekend. A guy's got to eat." It seems weird to call a boatman a taxi driver.

We load our kayaks on the flat, wide deck of his craft and settle in for the one-hour ride upriver. Our driver points out a few of the interesting features of Marble Canyon and gives a polite wave to each of the handful of small fishing boats sprinkled along the way.

We put our kayaks in the water just below the dam at 12:30 p.m. The skies are clear, the wind is calm, and the water is smooth. The trip is everything and more than I hoped for. The canyon here is a piece of paradise with towering, red sandstone cliffs. There are several small beaches for fishing, exploring, and relaxing. The water is clear and clean, unlike the muddy brown of the Colorado I've seen in canyon rafting photos. Muddy from all those overflowing Groovers.

The most famous feature of this area is Horseshoe Bend, where the blue-green ribbon wraps a 270-degree sweep around a massive red rock butte. Horseshoe is pictured in travel magazines worldwide. As we float languidly through Horseshoe Bend, it's only 2:30 p.m., and we're past the halfway point of the fifteen-mile float.

I gaze up at the cliffs towering 1,100 feet above the river. Hardy tourists can hike about a mile and a half across the plateau to stand at the precipice. There they can capture their own version of the iconic photograph. There are a couple of ants standing on the edge right now. This is our shot to be specks on the river in someone's award-winning *National Geographic* photo.

We should moon them. Nah. It's a family magazine.

I lean back in my seat, feeling pretty good about myself. Maybe I'm not such a hack amateur adventure guide after all. These guys are lucky to have me.

As we float out of the bottom of the horseshoe, I sense a slight change in the current. The river is slowing, but that's OK. We have at least three hours of daylight and only seven miles to the take-out. We've enjoyed a relaxing cruise on a lazy river, and it's still smooth sailing. We'll have time to park our boats and explore a couple of side canyons.

Not so fast, Beanie Boy.

I don't know whether we've been protected by the big bend in the river channel or if Trace's vaunted weather system is waking up from a morning siesta. The wind is definitely picking up. Thank goodness, it's only a crosswind. A quarter-mile downriver, it's quite a different story.

We arrive at the westward turn and are hit head-on by a howling fury of cold wind and spray. The formerly gentle green ribbon is overlaid with an army of whitecaps coming against us in a relentless onslaught. Each wave rises up two or three feet before landing a crisp *smack* against the bow, like the boss Stooge, Moe, delivering a sharp slap upside of Curly's dome.

At this juncture, the Grand Canyon is like a 226-mile long wind tunnel. Weird stuff happens in gale-force wind conditions. Cows fly. Rivers flow backwards, even rivers as mighty as the Mississippi. I've read about this rare occurrence, but now it's happening right here beneath my very butt. If I stop paddling only for an instant, I go backwards so fast it's startling. It takes everything I've got to creep forward at a millipede's pace.

Recreational kayaking is not overly technical, but there are a few tips a hack amateur adventure guide should know if he finds himself in a pinch. Let's see, paddling against gale force winds in near freezing wind chill conditions in rapidly fading daylight, does this qualify as a pinch?

Here's a tip even Gilligan Rube should know: there is no easy way to paddle against forty-mile-per-hour headwinds. Your best tool is time if you can afford it. Find a beach, park your boat, and wait for the wind to die down. Conserve your strength.

The utility of this tip assumes that any responsible boater has a dry bag full of essential stuff to survive a night in the wild. The Rube doesn't have on board a single item that could be called survival gear except a water bottle. And it's half-empty, like the Rube himself. We all know guys who are long on brains but short on common sense. The Rube is one of those rare individuals short on both.

Waiting it out doesn't seem like a good option. I figure as long as we stay dry, we can survive a night out here. People get in deep trouble when they capsize in frigid water and can't get to shore, an outcome more likely if we try to disembark in the middle of a hurricane. If we survive the dunking and the near-certain hypothermia, best case is we get out the next day with pneumonia. Certainly nothing to sneeze at either.

Now is not the time for mutiny, so Chad and Pierce agree to keep paddling until injury, exhaustion, or accident. All of which are possible. Then we reevaluate. Chad and Pierce are such loyal swabbies. They're going down with their skipper.

Chad is a good paddler, so he quickly puts some distance between us, and Pierce starts falling back behind me. After a half hour, there's at least a quarter-mile separation in front and behind. It never occurs to me, but allowing us to become separated is about the dumbest thing I can do right now. If one of us capsizes, nobody's going to know. Without an assist, it wouldn't be easy getting back in the saddle in the midst of this squall. A man can't function in water this cold for very long without a wetsuit.

I wonder what the boys are thinking about now. Forecast, schmorecast. Why should we listen to Trace? He's just a guy from a dive shop. It's not like he's some kind of prophet. Heck

Amos was just a plucker of wild figs. Oh, yeah, and a prophet (cf. Amos 7:14-15). But, noooooh, let's put our trust in Rear Admiral Rube instead. We should be lounging at the hotel pool back in Page right now.

After another hour of the frigid water crashing over my bow, I'm totally numb from the waist down. The water is a crisp forty-five degrees, but with the spray the wind chill is near freezing. There's plenty of time to pray, but not the mind to. Like other stubborn guys, I think I can do this myself. I don't need anybody's help. If things get really bad, then I might call on God.

I'm focused on the rhythmic power strokes required just to keep from going backwards. I'm thinking, *Seriously, how bad can it get?* We saw a few fishing boats below the dam earlier in the day. One of them can give us a lift or tow us in to Lees Ferry. The only harm would be our wounded manhood, but we're a bunch of city slickers from the Valley, so our manhood is suspect already. It's the strangest thing; the boats have all disappeared. Gone with the wind.

Chad is so far ahead he's out of sight. He's either mastered the intermediate eddy-hopping technique, or he's capsized and is on his way to dead. Pierce is also off the radar. The fellowship at the moment is just awesome. There is much to be said for the spirit of shared hardship. It sucks. But solo hardship is even worse.

My progress is excruciatingly slow. In a rare moment of relative calm, I stop paddling to rest. I lean over the kayak's edge and peer into the water. For an instant, I imagine the faces of Chad and Pierce staring up at me from below the surface, ghostly white corpses in the murky swamps of Middle Earth. I am responsible for leading Frodo and Sam to their watery Mordor. I am Schmiegel.

The late afternoon sun has dipped below the cliffs. Where Marble Canyon was chilling before, now it's downright ominous. Silence and seclusion are two of the best things to be found in the wild. Every man needs a place where he can be alone with his thoughts. There is a point, however, where silence and seclusion yield to fear for the timid soul. This is when many guys think about God for the first time. It's been nearly three grueling hours, when the little voice of doubt whispers in my ear, *Are we there yet?* No answer. Then a warning, *Like the fools of old, Rube, you disregard a prophet at your own peril.*

When the lights of Lees Ferry finally appear against the dusky pink cliffs, I'll admit to much nervous relief. All right I'm giddy as a Girl Scout on a sleepover. Not that I'm scared of the dark or anything. I feel a surge of adrenaline and suddenly my power strokes propel me like I'm in the log flume at Splash Mountain. Hold your horsepower, Popeye; it's not your awesome physical prowess. The river is suddenly completely calm. In an instant, the air has turned utterly still, and the water is like glass. It's as if a fickle finger just threw the cutoff switch on the wind tunnel.

For the last quarter mile into Lees Ferry, the tranquility is accented by only the riffle of my paddle and the crickets coming awake at sundown. Were the previous six and a half miles a devilish practical joke?

At the dock, I roll out of the boat on my hands and knees, shivering on the ramp, unable to stand upright on legs numb and wobbly. Chad has been ashore fifteen minutes already. After changing into dry clothes, he appears fairly normal. I must look like a survivor of "The Wreck of the Edmund Fitzgerald," staggering up the ramp. By the way, were there any survivors?

Fifteen minutes later I'm propped behind the cab of Chad's truck, shivering, half-naked, still struggling to change into dry clothes, when Pierce lands on the ramp. He looks every bit as bad as I do. It's 6:00 p.m., and night settles on this sleepy little outpost on the mighty Colorado.

The dock store is closed, but up the road the Marble Canyon Lodge and Restaurant is open. Chad leads us into the bar, looking like he could be a fisherman, resembling the other guys in the place. Pierce and I appear like a couple of wayward Eskimos bundled in layers of fleece and every article of clothing we could find.

The barkeep is gruff in a cordial way. "Beers for you boys?"

Chad is the only one able to speak without chattering. "No, thanks. Something hot. What do you have?"

The barkeep chuckles, "Oh, chilled, are you, mates? We got some firewater that will warm your innards. Scotch, Canadian, Kentucky Bourbon. What's your preference?"

I shudder, "Ssssswiss—"

"We don't have liquor from there."

I try again. "Swiss Mmmmmiss. Hot ch-ch-chocolate." The racket of my teeth chattering is like a jackhammer inside my head.

The barkeep waves his towel as if to sweep us from the bar. "You girls don't need me. You need a den mother. Let me get a waitress over here."

Maybe we're no better than a pack of quaking Brownies after all. Two and a half hours later, the shivering finally subsides.

But the chills are an indelible memory.

INTERLUDE: THE QUESTION, MY FRIEND

Months after our Lees Ferry adventure, I came across a column in a travel magazine warning readers that the Colorado River in Marble Canyon is extremely cold, so cold that fishermen have died just minutes after falling in the water. Good information. But better to know ahead of time, don't you think, Rube? God knows how close we came to the brink, and it's probably for the best that we don't.

It seems that hardships make a more lasting impression in our minds than the best of times. We feel validated as men if we overcome something difficult or potentially dangerous. If we bring it on ourselves through our own stupidity, it's more a salvage operation than validation. Still, we try to hang on to that feeling. Before a man can be a protector and provider, he first must be a survivor.

Hypothermia and potential drowning are but momentary inconveniences in comparison to the hazards facing our souls in today's culture. Are we ready for them? Or do we mostly rationalize them away? What are we doing in preparation and training? I prepared for our river trip like an afternoon at Big Surf. A responsible trip leader would have had more than a tube of sunscreen and a water bottle. Nice job, Rube.

A normal guy doesn't do a trip like this with the intention of putting himself through hell. He's hoping for a little slice of heaven. Our job is to be prepared for either outcome. Even when we're not ready, sometimes we escape unscathed. When we get away with a stern warning, it carries a responsibility to learn from the experience. Lesson one is thanksgiving.

We think we're masters of the universe when we subdue mighty rivers for our own purposes. Even with all our engineering genius, we're always at the mercy of forces controlled by a far greater power. A Boys' Trip adventure that goes off-script is a humbling reminder of our ultimate weakness and dependence. I've only lately given proper thanks for the mercies extended to this ill-prepared, unworthy subject with gratitude for holding back the rogue wave and diverting the rascally whirlwind that would have capsized us all.

When this tradition began, we didn't start each trip with a prayer of petition, and we didn't end with a prayer of thanksgiving. But we do now. Pray, tell; could these be the mustard seeds of elusive wisdom?

THRILL SEEKERS

Life lists are everywhere. It seems like every lifestyle, travel, and outdoor magazine has a special issue with their lists of the best places to go and things to see and do. Publishers and advertisers are smart. They wouldn't publish these if they weren't big sellers. People are looking for the thrill of a lifetime.

The Narrows of the Virgin River in Zion National Park is high on every worthy adventure life list. The Narrows is a darling of top photographers and advertisers, so it's likely you've seen pictures of it without knowing. Many call this classic canyon the most thrilling hike in the entire national park system. That got the Rube's attention.

A person doesn't have to be a serious hiker to get a taste of the Narrows. Casual tourists can get off the Zion shuttle bus and walk a mile on a paved path. From there, if the weather and the water flow conditions allow, they can wade into the shallow Virgin River and walk upstream between the towering canyon walls. No experience, equipment, or skills are required, just a willingness to get your feet wet and the ability to dream.

There's only one problem with this plan: trying to stay upright while wading against a swiftly flowing river on slippery rocks the size of bowling balls. No matter the time, the day, or the season, you're sure to have lots of company, but this is not necessarily a problem. If you wrench a knee or an ankle, there are plenty of people around to help. No offense intended, but a hike in the Narrows from the bottom up sounds like what a stadium Mass with the pope would be like. Maybe memorable, but not likely a moving personal experience.

The point of going to thrilling life list places is not just to brag on social media. It's to experience something that might help you become a better person. How is a man supposed to hear his inner voice, much less the voice of God, when the place is wall-to-wall with chatty shutterbugs? Such is the conundrum of a place too popular for its own good. Is it possible to hate crowds and still love people? It sounds like someone needs to become a better person.

Most folks are looking for the easiest way to do something, so a visit to the Narrows starts where the canyon ends in the middle of the park. To the Rube, that sounds crazy. Like reading the Bible for the first time starting with the book of Revelation. Don't laugh, I actually tried it. I just wanted to know how it all ends. I didn't want to be bothered with the nitty gritty. Anyhow, a life list trek ought to start at the beginning. Good thing for me, better hikers than I have already thought of that.

Like the intrepid explorers who first mapped the American west, adventurous trailblazers have tracked the Virgin River from its remote headwaters for sixteen miles through some of the most pristine, unspoiled territory in the country. Here is a trek for the determined thrill seeker, a worthy flagship hike. The Boys' Trip is supposed to be about training us for life, where we're going to have troubles. The boys don't need to know about the easy way.

The Hobbit drove solo from Montana and met up with Chad, Pierce, Kurt, and me in southern Utah. On day one, we toured around Bryce National Park, leaving just enough time to get down to Zion before park closing. Park Ranger antennae are on full alert when the Rube and his pals hustle into the Zion Information Center with barely a few minutes to spare.

The top-down Narrows hike is not widely known, and most visitors are discouraged from hiking it. If a guy insists on trying, the National Park Service requires a special permit and a briefing on the dangers of slot canyon hiking. Rangers are trained to recognize potentially hazardous individuals and are armed with a long list of risks and reasons for not doing the hike. These are the guys who must rescue unprepared or unlucky goobers or retrieve their unfortunate bodies out of the canyon. It's understandable that they would want to restrict traffic in the upper Narrows to only the qualified.

In winter, many parts of the Narrows get direct sunlight for mere minutes a day. It's cold enough to keep normal people out of the remote upper canyon until after the spring snowmelt. We're here in October, and they haven't had a Narrows permit request all week. Ranger Roy and his assistant are hoping the top-down Virgin River hiking season is over for another year. Not if the Rube has anything to say about it.

The boys poke around the center looking at the cool photos and other touristy stuff while I take care of the paperwork. I'm feeling lucky. "Howdy, Ranger Roy. How about a hiking permit for the Narrows?"

Behind the main counter Ranger Roy dons his helpful and courteous hat. "Howdy, yourself. You guys don't need a permit for the Narrows. Just take the shuttle to the end of Zion Canyon Drive and get out at the Temple of Sinawava."

I'm ready for that line. "Sir, we want to hike the Narrows top-down."

Ranger Roy is not through being helpful. He acts like he didn't hear me. "Everyone hikes up from Sinawava. You will love it. It's beautiful right now."

"I appreciate that, sir, but I've checked it out, and we'd like to see more of the canyon."

Apparently, I got through this time because Roy is beginning to bristle. "Oh, you've checked it out, have you? Well, it's possible to start at the north end, but you don't want to do that. The drive is long, and the road is rough, and you need to shuttle back the next day to get your vehicle. The canyon up there is really cold. Bottom-up is much nicer."

I nod and scratch my chin. "We don't mind a little difficulty, sir. Actually, we prefer a challenge," I reply, speaking for myself.

The Rube is not taking his advice, and Roy is starting to take it personally. "I don't think you know what you'd be biting off." He pulls out the Backcountry Planner from behind the counter, opens it, and points to the Narrows' trip description. "Read that for me." His tone has turned icy.

I slide the paper around and try to assume an air of respect for authority. I read aloud,

"The Narrows is not a trip to be underestimated. At least 60 percent of the hike is spent wading and sometimes swimming in the river. There is no trail; the route is the river. The current is swift, the water is cold, and the rocks underfoot are slippery. Flash flooding and hypothermia are constant dangers."

"Can I stop now, sir?" I ask meekly. "We know all that."

Ranger Roy is not amused. "Keep reading," he replies tersely.

I continue.

"Good planning, proper equipment, and sound judgment are essential for a safe and successful trip. Your safety is your responsibility."

Ray snatches the paper. "Now you can stop. I just want to make sure we are clear on that last point."

What's also clear is that the Rube is not to be denied, and Ranger Roy has expended about all his ammo. He tells me to gather the boys for the safety briefing.

After we endure a fifteen-minute tale of what can befall the unprepared in a slot canyon, Ranger Roy issues our permit. With a deep sigh and wry grimace, he logs our vehicle ID information. Then he asks to shoot a copy of my Arizona driver's license.

"What's that for?" I ask.

"Makes next of kin notification easier," he grumbles. Wise guy.

Bright and early tomorrow morning we're headed for the Narrows the hard way. This will be a test of the Rube's theory that thrills are way sweeter when you have to work for them.

We depart our Zion Canyon campsite in the dark. A ninety-minute drive on a rough dirt roads brings us to the Virgin River headwaters. When we make the turn on Chamberlain Ranch road, six white tail deer bound down the road in front of us. They tease us for a quarter-mile before vanishing into the high desert brush. This is so cool.

When we make the parking pullout at 7:45 a.m., it's a crisp 29°F. Glenn glances at the temperature gauge and mutters, "I've only got this one sweatshirt."

I reply, "No worries, Mayor Hobbit. We have a few miles of dry hiking before we hit the water, and it'll be warmed up by then." I hope. This gambit is all my idea, so I can't show any hesitation.

I glance down at Glenn's feet. I don't have any idea how he's going to do this wearing tennis shoes. But I should know that Hobbit feet are famously tough enough that shoes of any kind are optional. If they can handle Mount Doom, they can take this. Tennies will work just fine.

The sun has been up nearly an hour, so we have no time to kill. It's hard to estimate hiking speed in a river that varies from ankle deep to waist high for at least half of the sixteen miles. With ten hours of daylight left to burn, we're going to need every minute of it. I don't want to spend the night huddling under a rock waiting for Deputy Fife and his rescue team or the resident troll to return. I don't relish being regaled with a righteous *I told you so* from Ranger Roy.

The trek begins with a simple stream crossing on a single log lying across the shallow water. The boys make the stream crossing easily. It's only the Rube who bumbles off the log into the frigid water while fiddling with another piece of superfluous gear. This is just great. While the boys are traipsing along footloose and fancy free for the first hour, I'll be sloshing and squeaking with wet feet in sub-freezing temperatures. These guys have it way too easy. I'll show them what tough is. It's all part of my plan.

The first three miles are a gentle slope down the high desert floodplain following a rough ranch road. Small tributaries meander across the plateau, joining to form the artery that becomes the North Fork of the Virgin River. It's a brisk, pleasant stroll for the boys, a teeth-chattering slog for the prune-footed Rube.

At mile three we are funneled into the deepening canyon as the river begins its carving work in earnest. There's no avoiding the water now. The river is the trail. By mile six, the cliffs soar five hundred feet above us, and the narrowing canyon yields a hint of what's ahead. Soon the space between canyon walls will squeeze down to barely twenty feet, where direct sunlight lands for mere minutes a day.

The next few miles are the canyon's deepest, where the undulating sandstone walls will tower two thousand feet over our heads. On this day, the river is a gentle riffle over rocks polished smooth by eons of this gentle massage. The massive size of some of the boulders residing here, though, is a warning that sometimes the action is far from gentle. Our light and breezy conversation during the opening miles begins to yield to the depth of the growing stillness.

The Narrows is often referred to as a cathedral in stone. They no longer build churches like the historic cathedrals of Europe, but the Cathedral Basilica of Saints Peter and Paul in

Philadelphia exemplifies some of the majesty of the ancient sanctuaries.

On one of our family trips to the Philly area, Vickie and I made a sightseeing trip downtown to see the shrines of American Independence. It was Labor Day, and the city was teeming with the type of activity you find in a major metropolitan area on a holiday weekend. After a mostly frustrating experience with traffic, parking, walking, and crowds, I thought a visit to the Basilica might settle my nerves.

Once inside the church I noticed a curious phenomenon. People would be laughing, carousing, and carrying on until the instant they stepped into the narthex from the street. There was no usher, tour guide, or anyone there to shush them or give them a stern look or a wagging finger. There was just this amazingly beautiful place open to all with no admission fee, membership card, or restriction at all.

Visitors just immediately went quiet on their own. Even the rowdiest, most immodestly dressed, disrespectful characters got this look on their faces. Their eyes went wide, and their tongues fell silent. They may have entered the church as a gag or a dare, to make mischief, or just to cool off. Instead they behaved like perfect angels the entire time. There were no souvenirs, but perhaps they received something more valuable from their visit, an awareness in their soul that God is alive and available to them and indeed is calling to them in the quiet of their hearts. *Thanks for coming to spend time with me. Come back again real soon.*

I walked out of there refreshed like I just finished off a double scoop cone on that hot day. Yeah, the cathedral effect worked in Philly, and it's working big time in the Narrows right now. Many people believe God is never far from us, but even so we seem to need a sensual reminder now and then.

The Narrows is a deeply spiritual experience when your contemplation is accented by only the ethereal sound of your own footsteps in the shallow water. We allow some distance between us, so each guy can be alone with the grandeur. It seems sacrilegious to splash noisily or to run up on the guy ahead of you. My every step is stealthy, like I'm trying to sneak from the grandkids' bedroom after they've finally settled down for the night.

In this place, you can almost hear the thoughts registering in your mind and feel your soul stirring with the gentle riffle. Unless you have something deep or poetic to say, it seems blasphemous to speak. The five guys in our group are friends, but today the silent treatment is the biggest favor we can do for each other. A higher power has the floor. The Creator is speaking from his pulpit.

The setting of this trek redefines the term *solitude*. We don't see another soul for over eight hours, covering twelve miles of the most incredible terrain on earth. The river is flowing at a mild thirty CFS, so our hiking is not labored like a mid-thigh slog would be. We wade through a couple of waist-deep pools and skirt around a few others, six to eight feet deep. The pounding of a twelve-foot waterfall adds a crescendo to our soothing soundtrack. This is great fun.

Trekking among the soaring walls of sandstone, natural springs, hanging gardens, and stone grottos, has me thinking; this would be a great place for a Marian apparition. There is a deep, cave-like alcove covered with lush growth called the Grotto, and this is the Virgin River, after all. If he can't get contemplative here, a guy needs to have his temples examined, or rather, the space between them.

There are a handful of primitive camping spots along the river, but each one is as vacant as the Rube's expression when asked what's on his mind. On this day, we have paradise all to ourselves. God is giving us a private, behind-the-scenes tour on the making of a masterpiece.

Though it's hard to get lost following the river, this trek has its own brand of uncertainty and tension. To cover sixteen miles in the ten hours of daylight, we need to average over one and a half miles per hour. There are large stretches of the Narrows where we cover barely half that. The serenity is tempered by a nagging sense of insecurity that we aren't going fast enough to reach civilization before nightfall. I don't think I will have near the same sense of serenity in here after dark.

Not knowing what conditions are up ahead, it might be wise to pick up the pace. But I don't want to display any weakness or uncertainty. It's mid-afternoon when we pass the final campsite, and there are still no signs of civilization. Stress is in the air.

The Hobbit is a prudent soul, accustomed to pronouncing wise judgments and making sound decisions, so he takes matters into his formidable paws. He breaks into full MacArthur mode, takes the lead, and begins marching with veritable wings on his tennies. With the Hobbit exhorting us in a crisp drill cadence, our contemplative wander has become a purpose-driven march.

After an hour under full steam, we pass Big Springs when we encounter the first hiker wading upstream from the Temple. The Hobbit is our advance scout, and he queries our visitor. "How far out are we, amigo?"

"I left the Temple at 1:30. You've got a couple hours to go," he replies.

It's now 3:45 p.m., so we're on target for a 6:00 p.m. finish. Official sunset is at 5:50 p.m. We'll be safe and sound before dark. The good Lord willing and the crick don't rise.

For the final two hours, we're hiking opposite a growing multitude of waders splashing upstream from the Temple. I have to work at regarding them with charity rather than disdain and loving them, not despising them. That ought to tell you how far I still have to go in this soul-building endeavor we call life.

Upstream, the boys and I have been blessed to experience raw, unspoiled beauty in the priceless solitude of a privileged few. We were willing to put in the time, the effort, and even the sacrifice for the experience, but we in no way earned it. It was still a freely given gift. You'd think I would be a better man for having received it.

In the relentless pursuit of life lists and thrills, we're seeking the ultimate of all there is to see, touch, and feel here on Earth. Perhaps we're spending more time and energy worshiping at the altar of creation, rather than at the feet of the Creator. He is, after all, the source and giver of all that is good, true, and beautiful.

Far be it from me to point any fingers. Often the guy at the head of the parade of idols is me. I'm not dancing with joy at being in the presence of the Ark of the Covenant. I'm lifting high the golden calf.

INTERLUDE: HOW DEEP IS YOUR LOVE?

Bottom-up hikers in the Narrows can only go so far before they must turn back. The typical visitor sees at most only a quarter of the canyon, yet they check it off their life list. Such is our dilemma in the pursuit of excellence in anything, including virtue and holiness. How deep do we want to go? How bad do we want it? How much is enough? Usually, we're too quick to settle. We're too easy on ourselves.

The Lord has much more he wants to give us.

The top-down Narrows trip is like the spiritual journey of a lifetime. It can be risky, cold, and lonely. People will try to steer you away from it. The world will tempt you with an easier way. There will be times of fear and uncertainty when you want to turn back or bail out.

The beauty of the Narrows is nearly impossible to describe. It is something not merely to be seen; it must be experienced. The dramatic interplay of water, stone, and sunlight makes the Narrows incredibly intricate. More depth, detail, and color are revealed with each new angle of illumination. Sunbeams perform like paint brushes. It may take something supernatural to surpass this grandeur. Like, say, the face of God. With creation this magnificent, how much more beautiful must be the Maker?

LITTLE ALTAR RASCALS

The older a man gets, the more his boyhood memories tend to blend together. Their vibrant colors become worn and faded. Their sharp edges are rounded smooth. If he's not mindful, he might come to remember his boyhood as a forgettable, throw-away phase he simply survived in the process of getting on to bigger things. But the Rube thinks different.

The cornerstone of a man's character is often set in place during his early years. His lifelong concept of adventure is shaped by his boyhood experiences. These times are essential, not disposable.

A guy can't relive his boyhood, but he can and should revisit it. He might gain some insights on how he came to be the way he is. For the Rube, this is a scary proposition. I guess I was pretty much trouble right from the start. But I would have been a real problem child if not for Iron Man.

My dad was a disciplined man. My older brother, Weebs, and I would come to call him Iron Man. Dad must have known I was going to require extra disciplinary measures very early. He and Mom were going to need reinforcements. My conduct wasn't bad enough yet for reform school, but Iron Man figured if any paramilitary group were up to the task of reining in little Bruber, it was the Sisters of the Holy Roman Paddle.

Weebs and little Bruber wouldn't be attending the neighborhood elementary school like regular kids. We would be shipped downtown to parochial school. At much financial expense and sacrifice, Iron Man would nip this truancy in the bud.

Part of the deal of attending a parochial school was not just extra school work, but also the obligation to serve the church. We were taught that this was not a burden but a privilege and honor. The idea was to reorient our thinking from inward to outward at the very start, to turn us inside out. For boys that meant being an altar server at Mass.

There was a great deal of mystery to the altar serving program, so it was a mixture of curiosity and fear that kept me between the white lines, at least for a while. It seemed like we were being let in on a secret and admitted into an exclusive club, which was exciting. This seemed almost like an adventure. But we were just kids. What did we know?

At first, I managed to suppress my natural tendencies to make mischief, but it didn't take long for the newness to wear off and my impish inclinations to resurface. Just putting on the uniform didn't transform me into a cherub in search of a good deed. I was still a little rascal beneath a cassock and surplice.

Every school day at Saint Paul's began with daily Mass. A crew of four boys was scheduled to serve for the week, and we rotated through the four positions, each with different duties. The altar servers are supposed to blend in, to simply assist in the unfolding of the Mass without distracting from this awesome, mysterious event. We were taught to never intentionally bring attention to ourselves. Book was the one position that made us all nervous.

At the reading of the Gospel, the entire congregation stands, and all eyes are on the Book as he rises and proceeds reverently front and center, genuflects, climbs the four steps to the altar, picks up the Book of Scriptures from its stand, bows, carries the open book down the steps, faces the altar, genuflects again, climbs the steps, crosses over, and places the book on a stand on the other side of the altar. This ritual is very symbolic, and every gesture is packed with meaning. Maybe too loaded for a little altar rascal to carry.

This was not your ordinary book. The Book of Scripture was an ancient, ornate, massive volume that might have actually been the original parchment hand copied by medieval monks. To a kid, it was so bulky and heavy it might as well have been the Ark of the Covenant. No matter how many times a boy performed this task, the potential for disaster was ever-present. A number of things could cause a boy to crash and burn: a shoelace coming untied, a scuff on the carpet, or an ill-fitting cassock—the ankle-length, black garment we wore during the liturgy.

There were many close calls, but only one Book incident was worthy of *SportsCenter*; the time Monkey Man toed his cassock at the top step on his way down with the Book. Squatting like a Russian Cossack dancer, he remained upright for the first two steps, but by the third step he laid out in midair, like Barney Cipriani in a perfect swan dive from the cliffs of Acapulco. He landed with a *thud* that could be heard all the way to the choir loft. The air was sucked out of the place as the congregation gasped in unison. A collective murmur arose when Monkey Man jumped to his feet, his bent glasses hanging from one ear, and hoisted the scripture aloft like an outfielder displaying the ball after a diving catch. The sacred book never touched the ground. He was blind as a mole without his glasses, but the Word of God was intact. The nickname Monkey Man was due to his ginormous ears, which came in handy that day. He would get the game ball for the save, definitely a game changer.

Thereafter, we altar rascals would devise plots to trip up the Book of the day by untying shoelaces, unbuttoning cassocks, and other decoy maneuvers designed to distract his attention. Rather than being a bore, the mass was a source of adventure or misadventure if you were part of Bruber's crew.

St. Paul's two priests, McGuinness and O'Ryan, were both Irish but as different as Oscar Madison and Felix Unger. Monsignor McGuinness was tall and gaunt with jet-black hair. He preached in a monotone that reminded me of a croaking bullfrog, and seemed to me the embodiment of strict and humorless. Father O'Ryan was large and paunchy, and although he was the younger man, his hair was mostly gray. He was always a bit unkempt, his hair like a mound of mashed potatoes with extra salt and pepper. He was affable and easy going.

The best thing about serving Mass for Monsignor McGuinness is that he consumed very little of the wine in the course of the celebration, leaving at least half a cruet. After Mass, when Monsignor had departed, we little hooligans would pass the cruet around until all the evidence was consumed. As long as we shared the wealth, nobody was too wobbly to make it over to school on time. It was an early lesson in solidarity. We rise and fall together. On those days, first period was more interesting and amusing than usual.

Father O'Ryan, however, would quaff down all the wine with relish. In our eyes, though, he more than made up for it. At the completion of Mass, we would process reverently into the sacristy and kneel for a blessing. After Father blessed each of us individually, we assumed three-point stances, poised for action like miniature NFL linemen awaiting the snap. With a flourish, the stout Irish priest pulled his hand out from under his vestment and, with a flick of his fingers, scattered a pocket full of coins across the floor. A spirited rugby scrum ensued, as we clawed and pummeled each other for a bigger share of the spoils. Our pockets were jingling as we raced the three blocks downtown to Cottrell's Bakery.

Downtown was, of course, strictly off-limits during the school day, but we figured we had a dispensation since a priest had blessed us. We weren't sure how long the indulgence was effective, so we beat sneakers down and back. No matter how fast we flew, there were times when we were still late for first period.

"There was extra cleanup to do in the sacristy again today, Sister," was my standard excuse. "You know polishing vessels, folding linens, and stuff." The glazed donut residue clinging to the corner of my mouth was enough evidence to convict me. Bruber, you wicked, wicked monkey.

A tardy plus a white lie is called a combo, punishable by a day's detention and the added penance of cleaning the chalkboard erasers while everyone is at recess. I'm given the erasers for all eight grades, which is enough to build a decent-sized brickhouse. Since they hadn't fibbed, the other guys get off with a day's detention. But we are in this adventure together, so that doesn't stop them from helping me out. This was Christian brotherhood on display.

The approved method for cleaning erasers is to pound two of them together like an organ grinder's monkey clashing his cymbals. When I'd had quite enough monkey business, I thought hurling the erasers against the sidewall of the annex might provide a more thorough cleaning. I would be working on my fastball at the same time, an early version of multi-tasking. With some help from my pals, we turned the red brick annex wall into half a White Castle hamburger joint by the end of recess. That cost me a day scrubbing the annex wall, plus another day of pounding. I'm lucky my knuckles were spared the dreaded Holy Roman ruler. My pals escaped punishment because I never squealed on them. It's probably safe to say now, decades later, that Monkey Man was one of them.

In the days before the Second Vatican Council, Mass was said in Latin, and we were supposed to memorize the response prayers in Latin. Many times, we did what you do when you know the tune but not the lyrics. We would tell Father our humming was the groaning of the Holy Spirit. Facing away from the congregation to pray the Confiteor, we were required to profoundly bow. It quickly became a competition to see which of us would be the first to pop upright without drawing a penalty flag from Father O'Ryan. Five yards for offside, Bruber. *But Father, the tongues of fire were really flying today.*

The Latin prayers have long faded from memory with one exception, Mea Culpa. Mea Culpa. Mea Maxima Culpa. If you know any Latin, you know that's both appropriate and prophetic.

One of my few regrets is not realizing how much the chicks would have dug us if only we'd spoken a little Latin to them. It was much later that we learned that girls love mystery and romance, and there's a certain allure to a foreign tongue. I never dreamed of asking that cute girl if I could sit next to her on the bus, in Latin: "Excuse me, is that seat persona non-grata?" No, but the kid asking the question is. Carpe diem indeed.

It would take a lot more than a clever turn of a foreign phrase to remake little Bruber into a miniature Julio Iglesias. The sisters trained us to treat girls with respect. Girls were to be put on a pedestal. These nuns didn't put the fear of God into us for the heck of it. They were drawing from centuries of tradition and experience in handling hell raisers.

On a recent trip, my wife, Vickie, and I visited one of America's first Franciscan missions in Tubac, Arizona. The one-room school has been preserved as a museum, where we discovered a chalkboard dating back to 1848. On the board was a list of disciplinary infractions for the mission school kids with the associated punishment. At the top of the board was the most egregious offense, which drew twenty lashes, more than double the punishment for any other violation. The headline offense? *"Boys and Girls Playing Together"*. Yeah, these nuns knew what was best for us alright. Playing with girls is like playing with fire. But we never learn. Twenty lashes weren't near enough.

When we weren't serving, we found ways to make mischief as choirboys. Is there nothing sacred to little Bruber? St. Paul's is rich in history, featuring soaring arches, a huge pipe organ, and a choir loft about thirty feet above the nave. With the elementary school and a convent on campus, many of the nuns would retire at Saint Paul's when their teaching days were through. Even in retirement they would go to daily Mass. They were demonstrating to us that holiness is a lifetime pursuit. One such nun, I don't recall her name, so I'll just call her Sister, would sit alone in the back directly below the rail of the choir loft.

We all wore uniforms in those days, and the boy's uniform included a nappy green sweater with magic little fur balls. They were fruitful little buggers. No matter how many furbies we pulled off our sweater today, there were always plenty more tomorrow. Saint Paul sure wasn't Irish, so I don't know why our school color was green and our nickname was the Shamrocks. It was fitting, though, since we fashioned ourselves a mischievous clan of leprechauns.

Sister was getting on in years and was not as sharp as she had been. She may have been deeply immersed in prayer and contemplation because she barely moved during the entire mass. That made her an easy target for the army of tiny green paratroopers descending upon her from the boy's side of the choir loft. By the time communion rolled around, her shoulders and her black habit were fairly covered with little green, hairy hitchhikers. Sister was very small, so as she shuffled up the center aisle to communion, she looked like the *Peanuts* character Pigpen, trailing a small blanket of green dust bunnies.

The server holding the paten could scarcely contain himself. Monsignor McGuinness must have thrown a scowl in the direction of the choir loft, but we were too busy yucking it up to notice. We weren't so gleeful later that day when our backsides went under the Holy Roman paddle in front of the whole class.

The dark side of the adventure would take over on Thursday night when we would serve at Benediction. Saint Paul's is a Gothic-style church built in 1865 in the heart of old downtown. It was a far cry from the bland, generic churches typical in the suburbs today. Gothic architecture at night becomes an eerie and terrifying place to a kid with an active imagination. When I saw my first episode of *The Munsters*, I was sure they did the filming at Saint Paul's.

A narrow concrete walkway about two hundred feet long and barely ten feet wide separated the three-story red brick school building from the towering church. There was a light at each end of the alley, but at night the interior was really creepy, full of forbidding shadows and the sound of water dripping from somewhere.

Even though I didn't need to pass through the alley to get to the sacristy, on Thursday nights I would go through there anyway, just for kicks. I could start out skipping and whistling, but a quarter of the way into the murky shadows, I made a terrified sprint to the end of it. I imagined a hooded Vincent Price lurking wickedly, narrating scary passages from Edgar Alan Poe, while his long, gnarly fingers clutched at me from the shadows. Once safely inside the sacristy, sweaty and breathless, I dreaded opening the vestry closet door. The thought of Grandpa Munster hanging upside down in there behind the cassocks would haunt me for the rest of the night.

Over time, my vivid recollections of boyhood adventures began to fade. My growing worldliness led me to conclude that religion was not an adventure at all. I was becoming too smart for religion. Iron Man had been right about a lot of stuff, but he was wrong about this one. Religion was not worth the time and effort. It was boring and had nothing to do with exciting things like monsters, demons, or war. It wasn't about duty, battle, or a band of brothers. It had nothing to do with intrigue, mystery, romance, ghosts, and spirits. Religion was for children.

When I got out on my own, I was quick to let go of childish things like church. Now I was free to pursue important and exciting things like sports, cars, girls, and money. Yeah. That's when the real adventures would begin.

INTERLUDE: IRON MAN GIVES AGAIN

The job of being a kid used to be to have fun. Extra stuff, like school and religion, were things to be endured so we could get to the fun and games. Perhaps it's true that the man never completely outgrows the boy because, even as adults, many of us are ruled by an adolescent mentality.

As grown men, we think of life in competitive terms, as a game of winners and losers. In Western culture, the winners nowadays are comfort, entertainment, and convenience. Since the 1960's, religion has been losing. We're not just robbing from Peter to pay Paul. We're stealing from both of them.

Most of us from the baby boomer generation received some form of religious instruction as kids. It's not unusual for a boy to come to resent the religion of his childhood and even reject it as an adult. The path of faith for him becomes faint and overgrown, but still the soil of his soul has been prepared.

When everything in his life is coming up roses, he sees no need for anything or anyone beyond himself. However, when things are falling apart around him, a guy discovers that he's not as smart as he thought. Maybe it's not wise to rely strictly on himself. He's not that reliable. Perhaps he shouldn't always trust his instincts. His instincts aren't always honorable.

He might wander in the spiritual wilderness for years. But when the man starts looking for answers outside himself, he will come across the faint and overgrown path again. And it will feel familiar, comforting, and maybe even true. If he follows it to its end, he discovers an adventure more outrageous than even his childhood dreams. He might even recall an ancient teaching that as grownups we would need the type of faith we had as children (cf. Mt 18:3). What a concept—that one day we might be rewarded just for being kids again.

Past generations have passed down much wisdom to a generation that discards it too casually. Perhaps we think modern ideas are better, or that a thing isn't valuable unless we discover it ourselves. Maybe it's because we didn't have to work hard enough for it.

My boyhood religion was the map to a treasure that, once lost, would take nearly a lifetime to recover. I have no defense. Dad had always done what was best for us kids, often at great personal sacrifice. I should have known that he was trustworthy.

Iron Man had been right all along.

FOUR PEAKS SAKE

The full-blown Boys' Trip happens only once a year and for good reason. Comic mayhem exacts a heavy toll, so the boys need adequate recovery time, and our better halves need enough time to forget. In the interim, a day trip helps the boys stay connected. It might even help attract a new victim or two. Like sports, religious cults, and werewolves, a Boys' Trip needs new blood too. For a potential day trip, the Rube sets his sights on a wilderness area named Four Peaks.

Rising to 7,657 feet, Four Peaks is the highest point in Maricopa County, nearly twice the elevation of the Phoenix area's tallest mountain. Four Peaks hovers on the eastern horizon, visible from almost every hill in the north valley. Any hike destination is made better by a little intrigue, and Four Peaks has an air of mystery around it. Of all the places and products that take their names from it, it's the Four Peaks Brewing Co. that makes this mountain a patron saint in the Rube's book.

Brown's Peak, the tallest of the four summits, is not going to just roll over without a scuffle. Its rugged north face is split by a deep gash, 800 feet tall. This nasty scar is the only route to the summit. A prospective peak bagger must get his man card punched right here or get punched in the gut, and Brown's Peak is always in a fighting mood.

Technically, the peak route is a solid class 3 climb. Ratings are only subjective guidelines, however, and class 3 has a particularly wide berth for interpretation. Climb ratings are a bit like a common modern view of religion; every man is his own final authority. What is a simple class 3 scramble to a nimble hiker like my pal, Geronimo Jack, could be a class 4 deal breaker to me. A guy has to get out there and lay his eyes on a route, and then decide to put a boot on it or not. Either way, he's got to live with his decision or die with it.

Hikers have their favorite expressions for climbs like this, but they all agree on one thing: a guy should never do the Brown's summit chute alone.

I'm not a technical climber, but I've pushed the class 3 envelope once or twice with my pal, Milo. Never on purpose, mind you. If any of my hiking pals is capable of taming Four Peaks, it's the Gnome. He's always looking for a new challenge.

Milo works six days a week in landscaping, so time and energy are scarce resources to be conserved. Faced with extreme desert heat and dehydration, every workday for Milo is a race against the clock. This discipline carries over to his hiking. He aims for maximum efficiency with no extra weight or wasted motion. When I'm hiking with the Gnome, I often get the feeling he's holding back. He will let me lead, while he follows behind trying not to appear restless. He may be back there stopping every fifty feet to do a set of burpees. Most times, he patronizes me, sacrificing his workout for the sake of fellowship. For guys of different abilities to hike together, something's got to give, and Milo is one of the most generous guys I know. For an extremely goal-oriented guy, this is no small thing.

The drive to the Four Peaks trailhead is an adventure of its own. The casual sightseer might accidentally stumble onto the road to Four Peaks once before swearing, "Never again." The twenty-mile, chassis-rattling rumble feels like two hundred miles. The rutted, washboard forest road is good for something, though. It more or less guarantees solitude on the mountain. Tourists rarely make it as far as the trailhead.

The trailhead at Lone Pine is over a mile high, and the Brown's trail gains 1,200 feet in two miles. The official trail ends at Brown's Saddle with an expansive view that is quite impressive. It's a pleasant, moderate hike and a nice escape from the extreme summer heat in the valley. But that's not why we're here. Our mission is to confront the north face and to poke a finger in its eye. A gnome finger.

A trail conversation with the Gnome is an adventure in political incorrectness. He spends much of his workday on the road between client jobs, and he listens to a lot of talk radio. He's pretty well informed on the news, and on the trail, he delivers his version of unvarnished political truth with his own unique style. Milo's running commentary is frequently hilarious and always brutally honest.

The hike to Brown's Saddle takes about an hour, and that's where we get our first look at the craggy north face of Brown's Peak. Traversing the ridge toward the peak, the full impact of the gnarly, 800-foot beast is beginning to dawn on me. There's an odd gnawing in the pit of my stomach. Something tells me it's not the bacon, egg, and cheese biscuit I had for breakfast.

There's no trail to the base of the chute, just a sketchy route scratched out by a few hearty souls with an itch for adventure. To get a closer look, we'll have to scale the north apron, squeeze through a tight notch, and then creep along a narrow ledge cheek-to-cheek with the mountain. A slip from here would put an end to our day before we reach the starting line. The base of the chute is choked by a massive field of scree and a boulder pile, the product of a few million years of rock falls. It would be cool to see one of these behemoths come alive and rumble down the chute. Just not today.

After a bit of boulder hopping, Milo and I are at last standing directly under the summit tower, which has effectively snuffed out the autumn morning sun. The ravine is cloaked in a foreboding shadow that will persist for the next six months. Patches of snow and ice linger here into late spring even when valley temperatures are pushing 100°. Geronimo Jack knows of a fatality that occurred in this chute. I sense an eerie stillness here not born of peace. Our lighthearted fellowship is now a thing of the past. It's gut-check time for a pair of rookies.

This climb looks over my head, literally and figuratively. I turn to Milo, hoping for a shot of his usual optimism. His trademark impish grin has been rubbed out by a look of genuine worry. He admits to being nervous and suggests we pray. *Are you kidding me?* This is a first. We've hiked together for ten years and never thought we needed to pray about it.

Of course, Milo might just be concerned about having to carry me out of here on his back. He volunteers as a high school wrestling coach, so he knows what a dead lift is like. The Rube would be a load. Milo expects me to lead the prayer. I ask the Lord's guidance, not in making a wise decision, but in getting us to the top and back in one or two pieces. I've already decided we're doing it. I'm not driving two hours on a moonscape just to quit the minute things look a little dicey. Am I the only guy who makes his own plans without consulting God, and then begs for His blessing at the first sign of trouble? I'm old enough to know better. I can no longer fall back on the twin excuses of youth and ignorance, so I'll use the stubborn and macho cards I still have in my hand.

Physical strength, mental discipline, and patience are key skills in climbing. Not exactly the Rube's strong suits. I don't know much about technical climbing, but it sounds sort of like holiness. If life is a long climb to sanctification, it's best not to rush things in either case. Gain a little elevation at a time. Get accustomed to the altitude before resuming the climb. Become lazy or careless and you can lose it all at once.

I'm stashing my backpack for the summit climb when Milo asks if I brought any rope. A length of rope is a good idea at times like this, but I'd need to learn how to use it. I never made it past the first year of Cub Scouts. So, carrying a rope could make a hike more dangerous for the Rube. It could offer a chance for the boys to practice their hog-tying on me, or worse, fit me for a hangman's noose.

On this day, the climb goes without a hitch. None of the boulders comes to life, and Milo doesn't need the rope. The climb is challenging, but it's straightforward without the crazy peripheral exposure of a knife-edge ridge. After a forty-minute scramble, I clear the final obstacle and reach the summit where Milo is waiting.

His brown, furrowed brow gives way to a wide smile. "You're late! What happened, MacBruber? Did you have to defuse a bomb with duct tape and an envelope?"

I swipe off his bucket hat and rub his bristly head. Milo's thick, close haircut feels like one of his famously manicured lawns on bare feet.

"Remind me to talk to your barber. She missed a spot." Milo's wife cuts his hair. "Oh, and I used a Post-it note on the bomb."

After thirty plus years toiling in the desert sun, Milo's face is the color of my favorite childhood crayon, burnt sienna, the reddish-brown pigment created by roasting dirt in a furnace. I plop his hat back on.

"Now I have a question for you, Master Gnome. At the moment, you are the tallest guy in Maricopa County. How does it feel?"

His smile says it all. "Fabulous! Thank you for asking!" Milo is courteous to a fault.

Surveying the vast kingdom before us in all directions, I'm worried about getting down alive from this lofty perch. Gazing across the divide at the jagged profile of the other three peaks, anybody but Spiderman might regard them as untouchable.

On the bright side, the down-climb back through the ravine looks like a playground slide in comparison.

Before we head back, the Rube can't help but give the Gnome some well-earned advice from a clumsy tall guy. "Watch your noggin. It's a long way down from here, even for you."

To my relief, the return goes smoothly. When we reach Brown's Saddle, the imposing crag looming overhead looks different to me now. I'm in awe of the mountain, but I'm no longer paralyzed by it as I was two hours ago.

Yet it's time for some humility. Confidence is good, but too much of it is intoxicating. To regard myself as the mountain's master is to disrespect it. Arrogance in a veteran can be more hazardous than inexperience in a rookie. Good thing to remember for next time.

Reaching a summit makes the spirit lighter. The feeling of elation may be God's gift to enable us to return enthusiastically from the mountaintop and back to the trenches where we still have much work to do. On the way back, Milo is in a loquacious mood, as he tells me about a long-time employee who left him for what he thought were greener pastures. The guy has since returned, asking for his old job back. Milo says it's the parable of the prodigal son playing out in real life. The guy had been a good worker, almost like family, and Milo plays the part of Papa Gnome and welcomes him back with what he calls "overjoying whelm." Milo is of Swiss descent with German as his first language. He has an unusual way with English sometimes, but it's usually a poetic misspeak. I think I know what he means. He's a loyal, dependable employer in a cutthroat business, so to receive gratefulness and loyalty in return is especially rewarding.

In the prodigal son story, a guy could find himself in all three roles at different stages in his life. He could be the wasteful son, the obedient and jealous son, and the generous, forgiving father (cf. Lk 15: 11-32). At every age, we're each guilty of squandering our gifts and talents to some degree through cowardice, laziness, selfishness, or cynicism. The Rube has yet to cramp up from the overuse of a virtue muscle. Milo is not just more physically fit; it's a good bet he's in better spiritual shape too. A guy could take lessons in lifelong friendships and generosity from the Gnome. He doesn't just talk a good game, he lives it.

Milo works hard and long for everything he's earned, so naturally, he's skeptical of slick salesmen, silver spoons, and easy grace preachers. He cuts nobody any slack, especially loafers and freeloaders. They say education enables a man to work smarter rather than harder. But there's a certain nobility in manual labor that a guy will never earn parking his butt in front of a screen all day. Just knowing a guy like Milo makes me want to work harder.

To participate in the most challenging arenas of adventure, a guy rarely goes it alone. Divers have buddies, climbers have partners, and an ultra-runner has a support team. In the greatest adventure of his life, his struggle for heroism, integrity, and truth, a man needs a fellowship of brothers.

Whenever I'm in doubt, it would be good to ask myself, *What would Milo say?* My bet is it would go something like this: Set your goals higher than what everybody thinks you can do. Then give it everything you've got. You may not make it, but you'll be able to look yourself in the mirror with no regrets.

And you can count on Milo to be beside you, spurring you on. A guy couldn't ask for a better brother than Milo.

INTERLUDE: CAN I GET A WITNESS?

Men don't typically like asking for directions. In the business or professional world, a man will usually do all he can to solve a problem himself before he'll seek help or admit weakness. In his corner office, surrounded by a wall full of awards and other trappings of success, every guy is the king of his world. He's a self-made man. He'll figure stuff out on his own.

Get an office guy out into nature, and he's a different man. He doesn't have an image to maintain, a professional reputation to uphold, or a territory to protect. He doesn't need to demonstrate proficiency. He's not expected to have all the answers. A Boys' Trip is a chance for him to get a glimpse of a different, bigger picture and a new understanding of his place in it. Out in the wild he doesn't need to hide feelings of vulnerability, fear, doubt, inadequacy, or ignorance. They're not threats to his self-worth. The outdoor adventure may look like just another option on a guy's fitness menu, but it's really an invitation to fellowship and soul building.

Over a beer, a cigar, or a game, guys can talk for hours about trivial stuff: news, sports, weather, movies, cars, and guns. Blah, blah, blah. We're good at giving opinions about things that don't amount to much. But a lot of men are bad at sharing feelings. We tend to clam up when the conversation turns to deep, contemplative subjects. That's not necessarily a bad thing. The Rube's theory is that the sharing of feelings, has a time and a place. But it's not an essential task a True Man must do.

A man's vital duty is to testify to something with his life, first in action, then in word. *Testify*. The word implies strength and certainty. His testimony may or may not incorporate his feelings. A man's authentic testimony is dangerous because it wields great power. In law, it's the power to free and the power to imprison. In capital cases, it's the supreme power of life and death. It requires serious courage to go on the record publicly facing the deadly risks of retribution, reprisal, and revenge

A man's life is ultimately a long pursuit of virtue, and sooner or later he's bound to fall. It's in his nature. The testimony of other men is often instrumental to his turnaround. The witness of another can be a source of hope, encouragement, and ultimately life.

It's inspiring to hear from others who have stared down the same mountain and conquered it. Show me a guy who doesn't love a great comeback story.

A GRAND OLD MAN

"Cool, Nick. Sure. Lots of people hike the canyon in the middle of summer."

Crazy people.

Our son is on the phone. He tells me that he and his wife, Megan, are driving cross-country from California to Philadelphia. They'd like to stop in Phoenix on the way, and then drive up to the Grand Canyon.

Megan has never seen the canyon, and Nick's only visit was in elementary school on a field trip more than twenty years ago. I was a chaperone on that trip, and all we did was look into the big hole from the rim. Well, that isn't going to be enough this time. Nick has a bright idea that we should hike into the Canyon as a father-and-son adventure. I have taken two Boys' Trips into the canyon, so I should know what we're in for. The temperature inside the canyon is similar to that in Phoenix, which in July will approximate the surface of my pancake griddle.

Still, I'm pleased he would want to do a canyon hike with the old man no matter the season or weather. Though it isn't my idea, this excursion smells suspiciously like another of the Rube's half-baked schemes. I tell Nick he'll need to get the OK from the family risk manager: "Go ask your mother."

Vickie is likely thinking this plan sounds like a recipe for disaster. Combine one part youthful exuberance with one part middle age machismo and broil for eight hours. What do you get? Nuclear cheese crisp, an appetizer to die for.

It's one thing to risk the Rube on a Boys' Trip, but when her son may also be a victim, that's another story. I have a track record, though, since I've come back alive from two previous canyon trips. The third time might be the charm. The canyon can be a mixed blessing. Like apple fritters, Maker's Mark, and mom's meatloaf, it's possible to get too much of a good thing.

The canyon is considered one of America's most dangerous places to hike. An average of twelve deaths occur there every year along with hundreds of heat-related rescues. There are twenty or more cases of heat exhaustion every day in the summer. Most people have heard or read a Grand Canyon horror story of an unfortunate soul unprepared for the rigors of the big ditch.

Tragic misfortunes are no laughing matter, but despite the alarming statistics, there are good reasons why this junket should not overly concern a diligent family risk manager. First of all, people want to see the canyon. The more traffic, the more wrecks. Statistics can be deceiving. By the Rube's reckoning, the canyon is not as dangerous as it looks on paper

Many canyon visitors are Vegas tourists on a side trip from their gambling vacations. They are in no condition to hike, and most have no such plans. Once they arrive, however, they get swept up in the grandeur of the place. It's easy to stroll down the Bright Angel Trail and keep going. It's all downhill. Until it's time to climb out. Oops.

Since many foreign visitors don't read English, the park service does a good job with icon warning signs. One such sign is amusing. The sign for fall danger is the running stick figure turned upside down over the edge. It suggests that should you fall from the rim, keep your arms and legs pumping. It's doubtful that you'll hover to safety like a pelican, but you'll at least get to your final destination a bit faster.

You can't have a sign for every potential hazard. There are certain things that shouldn't require signs: wing tips, spiked heels, flip-flops, strollers, and wheeled luggage. These are items regularly seen in the canyon and are the same in every language: dumb.

It's the last week of June when Nick and Megan arrive in Phoenix. They will spend a day in the desert before making the four-hour drive north to the canyon. The temperature is expected to hit 110° in the valley today. It will be cooler at the canyon. On the rim, that is.

Shortly after pulling into the canyon, I collect the latest park information at the visitor center. The literature does a pretty good job when it comes to staying safe in the park. The list of hazards, supplies, and preparations to consider is long and thorough. I better keep this stuff away from Vickie. If she gets a hold of it, I won't be allowed out of the hotel room.

All the safety tips and suggestions can be summed up in one convenient rule: the moment you get out of your car, you're on your own. Before venturing into the canyon, a person better have at least the equivalent of the survival kit from the S.S. Minnow. Gilligan and those clowns survived three TV seasons with it. Miraculous. But those were simpler times. Do they sell idiot insurance?

Our visit starts with a stroll around the south rim with the girls. It's time for the experienced Boys' Trip leader to exhibit some of his hard-earned trail boss wisdom purchased with years of blood, sweat, and fear. I announce that any hiking should commence before sunup and finish by noon. That will give us the whole afternoon tomorrow to do touristy stuff with our wives. Good plan, Rube.

I tell Nick, "Drink extra water tonight, and get to bed early. Sunup is at 5:15. Let's get breakfast, and try to be on the 5:00 a.m. shuttle."

Nick has always had a mind of his own, and his own personal time zone: Daylight Burning Time. He pulls an all-nighter planning the rest of their road trip and shows up at our room at 7:00 a.m. I decide I'm not going to get agitated. This hike is for him. He should set the agenda.

I figure we'll hike down until we hit the halfway mark on our time, and then turn around to make it back up by noon. The general rule for a canyon hike is for every hour of hiking down, allow two for the hike back up. General rules are for generals, however. The Rube made it all the way to captain. A sensible rule like that may be above my paygrade.

Practically all of the tourists pound the dust down the Bright Angel Trail because that's what the park literature recommends. The availability of water and shade make it the safest option. A team of rangers patrols the trail in summer, prepared to assist distressed hikers. But Nick and I are seeking a wilderness experience, not a dusty human cattle drive, so we will avoid the Bright Angel. Instead, we'll take the South Kaibab, the trail less traveled.

The South Kaibab Trail follows the ridge tops rather than the canyons, so the views are unimpeded and spectacular. The downside is the trail is steep and exposed with no shade, no water, and no rescue rangers. The upside is that although we only have a couple of hours to hike, the South Kaibab will provide great views and solitude, a rare commodity in such a popular place.

We say our last good-byes to the girls and board the shuttle to the trailhead. We begin our descent at 7:20 a.m. The South Kaibab Trail leaves the plateau abruptly, zigzagging through a series of steep ledges carved in the rock. The first official viewpoint is called Ooh Aah Point, six hundred feet below the rim. Ooh Aah. Pretty much says it for the entire hike.

The terrain levels off at Cedar Ridge, where we pause to take in a glorious view of a formation called the Vishnu Temple. The canyon is a spiritual place. Very deep. If a guy were a superstitious type, he might expect a few spirits to still be hanging around what with all the deaths that have occurred here. The landmark names reflect an eclectic religious heritage. There are at least sixteen temples, several shrines, a throne, and a tabernacle.

"It's incredible to think that all of this was carved by a river," I muse, gazing at the vast palette of towers and buttes.

"Yeah, Dad, it's awesome," Nick replies. "But I've been thinking . . ."

You never stop being a kid's parent, so I've learned to hold my breath when a child of mine utters those words.

He resumes, "You can't say you've really been into the canyon without at least seeing the river, you know?"

I nod in agreement. "I'm not sure how much further before we can see the Colorado. But you're right. To come this close and not lay eyes on it would be a miscarriage of hiking justice."

From Cedar Ridge the trail is carved into the side of O'Neill Butte, a formation named after Bucky O'Neill. It would be cool for a man to have something permanent named after him. An office building would be OK, I guess, but the stone monuments in here have been around a couple million years. One of them would give a guy a measure of immortality on this side of eternity. If he were looking for that kind of thing. There's a rock called Hermit's Rest. What would a guy need to do to have his own place here? Rube's Roost has a nice ring; don't you think?

Our first view of the Colorado River occurs when we reach Skeleton Point, three miles and two thousand feet below the rim. I sense a bit of a letdown as Nick ponders the deep green ribbon in the distance. I can almost hear the gears turning in his mind.

"The river looks really small from here," he says. "I'm sure it's much bigger than it looks. It sure would be cool to actually hear the water. I'd be so stoked!"

"We still have some time," I reply. "Let's go to the end of the ridge and check it out from there." It's 8:40 a.m., and we're only a few minutes short of my turnaround time. I told the girls we'd be back around noon.

The guidebook says on a calm day you can sometimes hear the river from just below Skeleton Point. Something tells me that today is not going to be one of those calm days. At the end of the ridge, the trail plunges five hundred feet through a steep staircase of switchbacks. This is an all-or-nothing stretch. You can't stop halfway. Since we're not anywhere near tired, and it's not even hot yet, we negotiate the stairs briskly.

From the base of the stairs to the Tipoff, it's an easy stroll of a mile and a half on gently sloping terrain. Cake. The difficulty of this hike is so overrated. Forget the clock.

At the Tipoff, there's no doubt we can hear the river. But what's that? Along with the distant riffle I could swear I hear a small voice in an ever more insistent whisper, "Come to the water."

A park employee who is hiking on an intersecting trail is resting at the Tipoff.

"Make sure you guys have enough water," he tells us. "Sometimes they stash some in the hut over there. But there's none there today." Good advice.

"I think we're OK," I reply. "Thanks."

I'm not aware that Nick left half his water bottles in the shuttle van.

At 9:20 a.m., we watch the guy hike west on the Tonto trail. It will be more than six hours before we will see another living, walking creature.

At the Tipoff, the trail plunges 1,500 feet through the inner gorge for the final two miles to the Kaibab suspension bridge. At Panorama Point, a half mile down from the Tipoff, we have one more decision to make. Here is where the two suspension bridges, the Colorado River, and the Bright Angel Creek delta, appear. If there is an image of the gateway to the mythical Shangri-La, this is it. The die is cast. It's Rubicon or bust.

We skip merrily down the steep switchbacks like we're on our way to grandmother's house. We reach the Kaibab suspension bridge at 10:30 a.m., and it's only a short spur trail down to the rocky beach. We drop our packs in the shade of the bridge, and I empty a quarter-cup of red sand from my shoes. Soaking our feet in the frosty Colorado River, we go from bliss to throbbing numbness in thirty seconds. Numbness will be a fond memory about a half hour from now.

The South Kaibab gains nearly 5,000 feet over six and a half grueling miles. Funny, the miles weren't at all grueling on the way down. Oh, and it's 112°F in here today. In addition to gruel, deep fried rhubarb is on today's menu.

It's easy to see how an amazing environment can become intoxicating. On the way down legs are fresh, it's not too hot yet, and each successive viewpoint gets more enchanting. The prospect of the refreshing water is an enticing reward. A prize at the end of a hard test has always been an effective motivator. The problem with our particular scenario is that the reward comes first. We are now in debt, and payment is due.

This old dog and his puppy are facing six hours of sucking hot air and staring at nothing but dusty shoe tops. If all goes well. The theological concept of redemptive suffering says that suffering is not all bad. It can have value if offered to God for the benefit of another. But what if you bring the suffering on yourself? Is there anything redemptive about that?

The gray rock in the lower canyon absorbs and radiates heat like a cast iron frying pan. When thermometers read 112°F in the shade, hikers endure temperatures twenty degrees higher on the trail. That means 132°F. I should have brought some eggs.

I pick up a triangular piece of gray shale from the beach. I put the rock to my lips and imagine it's my official *Star Trek* transporter thingy. "Kirk to Enterprise. Beam me up, Mr. Scott." No response. "Kirk to Enterprise. Come in Mr. Sulu." Nothing but hot air. "Mr. Spock, prepare the mind meld." Precisely nothing, Captain. I clear my throat. "Ground control to Major Tom." I'll try anything.

We start back, on foot, at 11:00 a.m. Nick is considerably faster, so he trudges ahead looking for a sliver of shade to rest in while he waits for the old man. Every few hundred feet, I catch up to find him lounging in the crack between two boulders, like an oversized, reddish-pink chuckwalla. I get into a stop-and-go routine of hiking full speed for sixty seconds, then doubling over, hands on my knees for a minute or two, fully gassed. And then doing it again. Times five hundred.

There is a profound justice in the Grand Canyon experience. The transaction makes perfect economic sense. On the way down, each successive waypoint provides a higher level of enjoyment. On the way up, every marker exacts a correspondingly higher toll. We know in advance what the price is, and we're prepared to pay it. Haggling might make a guy feel better for trying, but there are no discounts to be had.

At about halfway sits that torturous stack of tight switchbacks, five hundred feet tall, called the Red and Whites. Nick renames them Lucifer's Lunges, which reflects our collective state of mind at the moment. Maybe it'll help me power through them if I imagine crushing the head of a serpent with every long stride. Instead of the fleet-footed St. Michael the Archangel, however, the shuffling tempo of a sputtering locomotive is about all I can muster. *In the muffling sadness . . .*

Now seems like a good time to recall what the park guidebook says about how Skeleton Point got its name. The bones littering the bottom are not from hapless hikers, but pack mules that slipped over the cliff to be reduced to whitewashed relics in mere days. There's also a diagram of the canyon geology with the different layers of rock. It looks hauntingly like Dante's vision of the seven levels of Purgatory. Nobody actually dies in Purgatory, although I guess it can get pretty bad. But at some point, a soul knows it will be set free to go on to better things. Like Paradise. The earthly inferno of the canyon in full blistering summer, meanwhile, is different. People and mules actually croak here on days like this.

Despite what you've heard about stupid tourists doing dumb tourist things at the Grand Canyon, we can't find a single other stupid tourist on the trail today. Nick and I look at each other. We are them. There is time enough to pray a year's worth of Rosaries, but the thought doesn't occur to me. The stillness is absolute, but for my every labored footfall on the dusty moonscape. Fine red powder permeates everything. It will linger in my white shirt even after years of machine washings.

During one interlude, I spot a wild California condor soaring above me. I haven't seen Nick lately, should I be nervous? Isn't a condor a type of vulture? Yes, a very big vulture, the biggest flying bird in the Western Hemisphere. And damn ugly to boot. If he gathers his friends and they begin circling overhead, this is not a good omen. Oh, man.

Where the way down was breezy and carefree, every step on the way up requires a concentrated effort. My mind is totally occupied with putting one foot in front of the other. It's good to think about stuff we usually take for granted. To be mindful of something as natural as walking helps a guy to appreciate the simple things. I think of a Cursillo buddy who has multiple sclerosis. The acts of standing and walking can be an ordeal for him, but he refuses to surrender to the wheelchair. He's determined to not let his illness run his life. He insists on being treated the same as any other guy on the team. The Cursillo retreat requires much manual labor, and he gets in there, always cheerful and encouraging, and does more than many of us. Then he tops it off with a solo *Late*

Nite Catechism performance as Sister Mary Baltimore in full nunnery regalia. He brought the house down. Maybe I can be like him someday. I hope it doesn't take a heavy cross like MS to do it.

It's 3:30 p.m. when we finally see signs of life; A couple of day hikers from the South Rim. They look at us like we're from another planet.

"Where did you guys come from?" one of them asks.

"We're from France," I want to say in my best Conehead imitation. But I haven't the strength. I tell them where we've been, and they are shocked and awed. Yep, we are the ones who are doing what everyone says can't, or at least shouldn't, be done. But, hey, guidebooks, rules, and warning signs are for the average guy, and we are anything but average. I for one am well below.

His partner is trying to encourage me. "You look like hell," he says.

The next hiker to pass exclaims, "You guys are my idols!" He turns to his partner and says, "We are doing it tomorrow, rim to river and back the same day!"

Great. Now I will have his death on my conscience. But I shouldn't worry. If he's like most guys, the momentary bravado will pass, and he will return to his senses. He will go home tomorrow and tell his friends he hiked the canyon, and no one but the hard-core fitness freak will care how far or how fast.

I better soak up this adulation while I can. If any of my newfound admirers happens to look back after they pass, my survivor man persona will vanish faster than a snow cone in Phoenix. It's a pathetic sight, me doubled over, tongue dragging in the dirt, sucking air like the wheeze of a cheap harmonica. Not exactly a picture of athletic prowess. I am one whipped dog right now.

The final stack of switchbacks below the South Rim is called The Chimney. Nick is up ahead, and I am just below the tower of Z's carved in the limestone. The increased flow of day hikers streaming down from the rim is starting to cramp my style. I have a vain image and a reputation to uphold. I don't want to look like I'm on my last legs, so I forego my usual stop and go routine. I push relentlessly without a break until I'm only a hundred feet below the rim. Very impressive.

I'm on the very last switchback when I pause to compose myself for the crush of paparazzi that awaits me on the rim. The famous slow-motion beach running scene from *Chariots of Fire* is playing in my mind. This is going to be classic. Suddenly my fantasy freezes like a bad rental DVD. My legs have decided that they are no longer part of the program. Five hundred times they have obeyed my marching orders. We are this close, and they choose now to mutiny. I don't have a leg to stand on.

Without warning, my legs dissolve from under me, and I fall like a dust-covered bowling pin. I bounce twice and throw my arms out to keep my legless torso from rolling down the trail. I'm in plain view of at least twenty people up on the rim, but they must think I'm clowning around because nobody is rushing to my aid. The Rube's reputation precedes him even here, it seems. He's grappling with an imaginary serpent again, or more likely tangled in his own bullwhip.

I struggle to sit upright as if I'm taking in the view one final time. Meanwhile, Nick has been up on the rim for at least ten minutes, probably signing autographs. I'm talking sweetly to my legs, telling them that everything's going to be OK. I promise I will never make you do another burpee for the rest of our life if you will just start working again. After a few minutes of this silent dialogue, a tour van driver and his associate walk down from the rim.

I strike my best Rodin's Thinker pose and pretend I don't see them. I am thinking, after all. I don't need anyone's help. I am not helpless. Whatever this is will soon pass.

The driver waves his hand sheepishly in front of my face to break my spell, and says, "You're not OK, are you?"

I snap, "I'm fine. There's a really cool caterpillar down here. Of course, I'm OK. I mean, I'll be OK."

His associate says my situation looks similar to an incident that happened to him once when he was running a marathon.

"You like caterpillars too?" I asked.

He recounts how he was within shouting distance of the finish line when his legs decided a marathon was twenty-six miles, and not 26.2 miles. He flopped on the ground helpless. He ended up dragging himself on his elbows the last two tenths of a mile in forty-five minutes. Poor guy. But he finished a marathon, and no one can take that from him.

Stubborn, proud Rube is not ready to surrender. I'll finish this mission caterpillar style before I let these guys carry my carcass off the field on my shield. Mentally I've made the transition from *Indiana Jones* to *Gladiator*. This is war now.

The associate then says he discovered later that his condition, called hyponatremia, was caused by a low level of sodium in his system, brought on by long periods of intense sweating and not replacing the lost electrolytes. He goes up to the rim again and comes back with a couple bags of salty snacks and a Coke.

"Try these and see if it helps."

"Thanks," I reply. "You're a Good Samaritan to this weary traveler."

I don't think to ask him if I'm still in this same spot by nightfall, will he come back and tuck me in?

Human body chemistry is amazing stuff. Five minutes after disposing of the snacks, my legs are back in the game, and I'm walking up the trail on pure pretzel power. I'm trying to put on my best *Saturday Night Fever* strut, but I must look like I'm fresh from an audition for *The Walking Dead*.

Having just experienced trailside mercy, I'm bracing myself for the fitting trailside justice I deserve. Too bad there is no ranger on the rim to administer a righteous public scolding.

The canyon, or any serious hike, demands a particular level of respect. But disrespect, selfishness, and borderline arrogance were on exhibit in our escapade. Ever the optimist, though, now that it's done, the Rube sees it as a learning experience and an opportunity for repentance and reconciliation for the offenders.

Just as important, it's a chance for those offended to extend forgiveness and mercy, in short, to be like Christ. All this time I was thinking about what's wise and prudent and what's good for the girls. Right, Rube. Seriously, Vickie and Megan showed Nick and me a level of selflessness worth striving for.

They waited for hours in the heat, disappointed time and again with each empty shuttle. They went from annoyed and angry to anxious and afraid and back again. They prayed for our protection and safety. And then for justice. They're not saints. Yet.

While I'm grateful there is no statute of limitations on the Lord's forgiveness, I hope for all of our sakes he doesn't change his mind about the depth of his mercy. Fortunate for me, we know it's at least as deep as the Grand Canyon.

INTERLUDE: MAN UP!

As long as there are trophy hikes, there will be trophy-seeking men.

I was man enough to finish the entire canyon trek against all manner of advice and warnings, but I wasn't man enough to be the responsible adult. Not man enough to put my foot down and say enough, no further. To abide by the wisdom of those who have passed this way before. To draw a line in the sand and then enforce it. A True Man doesn't jeopardize his son's well-being to be his crazy, rebellious, fun-loving pal. He stands firm as a loving, responsible father.

A Boys' Trip succeeds to the extent that it builds virtue, not when it glorifies foolishness. Our grand adventure is not a testament to manly strength and endurance in pursuit of a trophy hike. It is, above all, a tale of mercy and forgiveness, both human and divine.

But it's something more. It's a vivid reminder that every heroic virtue is the flip side of a deadly vice. Being two sides of the same coin, the virtue is never far removed from the vice. Humility is never safe from becoming false or prideful.

While we're never far from failure, it's encouraging to know we're always nearer to forgiveness and another chance.

ALONE, ALONE ON THE RANGE

Geoff has been our bug man for over twenty-five years. During that time, he's had experience with just about everything, including a few of the ten plagues of Egypt. Fortunately, not all at our place.

We can rely on Geoff to be on time and on task. Except as it pertains to bugs, he doesn't talk much. Geoff has a friendly face, a gleam in his eye, and a spring in his step. He is thorough and never in a rush. When he shows up at our house, he's a man with a purpose. Never once has it seemed like he would rather be someplace else, or doing something else. How refreshing, a bug man who just wants to be a really good bug man. Very old school. Geoff doesn't know it yet, but on his next visit to our house, he's about to encounter an entirely different type of pest—persistent, annoying, frequently offensive, and immune to everything but the sole of a good stiff boot.

In the course of daily business life, we deal with too many slackers, whiners, and complainers. We don't get to work with enough guys like Geoff. Geoff is a glass-half-full type of guy, and everyone could use a little more of his kind of optimism.

In one of the Rube's rare epiphanies, I get the idea that after all these years, I should get to know Geoff. It would be good to find out what makes him tick.

As usual, Geoff arrives at our home for our bi-monthly service five minutes before his scheduled time. Vickie meets him at the front door. Rather than remain quarried in my cave like usual, I come out to the kitchen and try to strike up a casual conversation in my uniquely clumsy style.

"Hey, Geoff. Is that a new hat?"

Geoff removes his cap, looks quizzically at it, and puts it back on. "Uh, no. I've had this hat for twenty years or so."

"It looks good on you," I offer. "You should wear it more often."

No doubt wondering about my newfound chattiness, Geoff casts an inquisitive glance toward Vickie as if to ask, "What's gotten into him? He's a regular Doctor Phil."

It takes another couple of visits, but once he gets used to the idea, Geoff is receptive to the whole talking concept. I must be careful not to call it "sharing." No guy enjoys that.

Over the course of a few months, I learn that Geoff is an avid hiker who is out in the wilds of Arizona just about every weekend. He does what most experts say not to do. Geoff hikes alone. Occasionally, he will lead a local hiking group on a day hike, but mostly Geoff hikes by himself. He's not antisocial; he just likes to go off-trail, take his time, poke around, and explore. Geoff is, in his own words, a dawdler. He likes to set his own course and his own schedule, often going out on the spur of the moment.

I'm excited to know that we have something else in common besides both being unusual characters. "Sounds like you're an explorer, Geoff. Where are your favorite places to go?"

Geoff closes the hall closet door and gives his sprayer a pump. "Skull Mesa, the Superstitions, and up north on the rim in summer. Once a year, I'll take a backpack trip for a few days with a couple of guys, usually to Colorado."

My elf ears perk up. "That's cool, Geoff. I take a few guys out somewhere every year, too. We should compare notes."

I have a feeling there's a lot I can learn from him. Maybe something to help the Rube lead a better Boys' Trip. The feeling is probably not mutual.

Geoff is an accomplished horseman who has worked a few ranches as a cowboy in his day. He was married once, but it didn't work out. He has a daughter, but he doesn't talk much about her. I'm surprised to find he likes to play golf. Geoff doesn't fit the country club profile. He sports a thick mop of hair he keeps tucked under his ball cap, except for the shoulder-length ponytail that falls out the back. With his unruly Mark Twain mustache, he looks more like a greenkeeper than a card-carrying club member. If he wanted to belong, he'd wear a pair of tight, loud, plaid trousers. But Geoff isn't the type of guy who seems concerned with image or putting on appearances. Geoff is all business, a no-nonsense guy.

If you asked Geoff, he would tell you that he doesn't have a story anyone would care about. Nobody would be interested in just another average guy. But I don't believe that. Geoff is a throwback to an era when humble character and integrity were the default settings of men. I'm not sure if it's like that anymore.

Geoff is into minimal hiking, which involves multi-day treks with lightweight, high quality gear. No frills, just essential stuff. He's very particular about the fit, weight, and durability of his equipment. Once a year, Geoff goes to a big trade show in California at the kick-off of the Pacific Crest Trail hiking season. This show is the only place where he can try out all the best minimalist equipment in person. Online shopping is not personal enough. Geoff needs to take the measure of a piece of gear by laying his own hands on it.

Being a self-employed business owner with no employees to cover for him, Geoff has only one day free to make the drive over to California and back. But this day, a client calls to report ants in his kitchen. Geoff could have told the guy to go down to the hardware store, get a can of Raid, and wait for him to come out Monday. Instead, Geoff cancels his plans and takes care of the ants on Sunday. Unless the red ant army chews through the pantry wall and is advancing on junior's bedroom, I can't imagine this being a dire emergency requiring same day, weekend service. But that's just the type of guy Geoff is. The client always comes first. Old school. When I was a small business owner, I tried to be like Geoff.

As a hiker, I don't think I'm much like Geoff at all. I wouldn't think of trekking long distances off trail in the wild. I always have a goal, a specific trail, or a target destination I'm aiming for. My plan is to be of out of the wild with daylight to spare. It sounds like Geoff hikes just to be out there, as far away from the world as possible. I'm not sure I could do what he does.

I follow Geoff on his brisk walk through the house: opening closet doors, spraying baseboards and behind furniture. "I'm just curious, Geoff; when you go for a couple of days at a time, what do you do out there by yourself?"

Geoff's manner of speaking is deliberate, plain, and direct. He doesn't use extra words when fewer will do. "I come across all kind of interesting stuff, petroglyphs, mineshafts, old prospecting equipment, forgotten ruins, real pieces of history. People in a hurry don't know what they're missing. You have to go off trail and poke around some."

Geoff caches extra water for the hike back and packs light, so he can carry out any cool stuff he finds. "I hauled a length of heavy chain out one time," he recalls. "Must have weighed forty pounds. They don't make chain like that anymore."

Listening to Geoff, I'm thinking, *They don't make men like Geoff anymore.*

"Isn't it a little risky being alone off the beaten path?" I wonder aloud.

Geoff shakes his head, "Not if you know what you're doing."

I keep poking, "What's the strangest thing you've seen out there?"

His reply comes pretty quick. "One time out near China Wall I came across the biggest rattlesnake I've ever heard of . . . big around as my arm and near seven feet long."

Geoff couldn't just leave him be; the snake might terrorize the next hiker or horseman that happened by. I don't know how a guy sneaks up on a monster like that, but Geoff did. He backed away and then came around undetected behind the snake and, using his hiking stick, tapped it lightly on the head. The snake just fell over, like a believer at a Benny Hinn revival. Geoff proceeded to dispatch the drowsy beast with a big rock. I have never heard of such a thing before. I have no reason to doubt Geoff until I learn that he's also a fly fisherman. Everybody knows fishermen are more likely to be liars than not.

Geoff doesn't seem to be in a particular hurry, so I keep going. "I'm not a fan of hiking cross-country like you do, Geoff. It seems like I get in trouble the minute I go off-trail."

I tell Geoff about hiking with my pal Chad on the Barnhardt trail in the Matatzal Mountains. We're aiming for a seasonal waterfall about three and a half miles in, but it's late spring, so we're not surprised that when we get there we find the stream barely a trickle across the trail. Still, we ought to at least check out what remains of the falls to make sure it's not just a legend of the falls. Geoff is a fan of corny jokes and bad puns. He gets it.

Leaving the trail, Chad and I start working our way up the streambed when I spot a small cataract a short distance off the trail. It's more like a shower, but very nice, especially now that the day is warming up. The water is flowing over a lip about sixty feet up the face of the mountain. There's no trail up to the pool, but there's evidence that someone or something has at least attempted to climb up there.

The rusty gears in the Rube's mind begin creaking. Why settle for a shower when you can take a dip in a pool on the side of a cliff with a cool view? Chad has been through enough with me to know when I've made my mind up to do something, he's not likely to change it.

Before he can say, "Yep. Yep. Yep," I'm working my way through some gnarly brush up a hill littered with boulders, loose dirt, and cactus. I'm less than a minute into this off-trail scramble and daydreaming about how this could be another of the Rube's classic Arizona adventures. The slope is about fifty degrees, and when I reach toward a surface boulder to steady myself, I'm staggered by a shrill, bloodcurdling squeal inches from my face. I jerk my hand back, as if jolted by a live power line, and nearly tumble down the hill. A thick, reddish, leathery body slithers under the boulder.

I had been within an arms-length of a tiger rattlesnake. I'm told that rattlers vary the intensity of their rattle based on the level of danger they perceive. This sound was not a cutesy little Pebbles baby rattle. It was scarier than the wickedest viper Indiana Jones ever tangled with. I'm supposed to believe the snake was scared of me? That's very funny. The Rube is indeed dangerous but only to himself.

Now I'm wobbling precariously on a steep, prickly incline, my whole body shaking, too afraid to take a step. I let fly a few choice words, one of them was "holy," but the others aren't "alleluia," "brother," or "amen." I holler at Chad who is twenty feet down the hill. I won't move until we verify the snake is back in his den.

I feel like an idiot. I am an idiot, albeit a lucky idiot. This spot is a rattler's paradise. It has everything a snake could want: fresh water, a cozy den, and for entertainment the occasional stupid hiker.

On the trail that morning Chad and I had discussed whether we'd ever experienced one of those times of great peril when your life flashes before your eyes. Chad said it happened to him only once when he was in the middle of a horrific, high-speed, dirt bike wreck. He escaped with only a few scrapes and contusions. His bike didn't make it. I've yet to have the classic, "Rube, this is your life," flashback experience. Maybe with a little more practice doing stupid things.

When I'm able to move again, I've forgotten all about the pool. The cool shower will do just fine.

All the while, Geoff is listening patiently. He nods like he knew where this story was going all along. But I'm not done yet, "You know, if I were you, Geoff, hiking solo and struck by a rattler, several hours from an emergency room, I might have been in deep trouble."

Geoff grins and winks, "You're not me. I wouldn't get myself into a fix like that. You should try using your head for something more than a blunt instrument."

It's a good thing Geoff always has a twinkle in his eye. A sensitive guy might be offended.

You don't get to be as wise as Geoff, however, without getting yourself out of some situations. I wasn't going to let him off that easy. I press him, "Do you ever worry about getting lost? I guess you probably have GPS now like everybody."

His response startles me. "GPS doesn't make you smart; it makes you stupid. I have no use for it." Geoff goes on to expound that rather than making a person safer, GPS can make a hiker more dangerous. "A lot of people are pretty dumb anyway, but because they have GPS, they put their brains in sleep mode. Technology's a crutch that makes them even lazier."

According to the gospel of Geoff, the essential tools for the serious hiker are the hardcopy topo map, a magnetic compass, and a Post-it note. He says, "That other stuff is optional. Make sure what you bring is worth its weight. Simpler is almost always better. Fewer things to go wrong."

I wonder if he realizes he's just affirmed a variation of a medieval theory of philosophy, Ockham's razor. There are plenty of cowboys in the arts: writers, poets, singers, and painters. Geoff could well be a cowboy philosopher.

And he's not finished expounding. "Oh, and I always have a deck of cards, so I don't worry about getting lost."

Now he's really got my attention. "Shut up! How does a deck of cards help you if you're lost?"

Geoff grins. "If I'm not sure where I am, all I have to do is start a game of solitaire. I know as soon as I get stuck, somebody will show up and tell me to play the red seven on the black eight."

With that, Geoff is out the front door and headed to his truck. And I'm left shaking my head.

He stops halfway and turns. "You didn't ask about the Post-it note." He doesn't wait for my reply. "Always leave a note where you're going." He adds with a twinkle, "Or in your case, where you think you're going."

My lie comes so fast, it's scary. "I never go anywhere without doing that." I wonder what the punishment is for breaking one of Geoff's commandments.

I follow Geoff out to his truck where he is prepping his backpack sprayer. I notice a small pile of books on the front seat. "I didn't know you're a reader, Geoff."

He shrugs. "Customers are always giving me books. Once in a while, I'll take a small paperback on an overnight. Nothing too heavy. Can't let it weigh me down."

I wince. "If I tried to do what you do, Geoff, I wouldn't sleep a wink in a tent in the middle of nowhere. The silence and being completely alone would freak me out. Having a book might make it a little easier, though. What are you reading now?"

"A customer just gave me *Unbroken,* and I've been devouring it. Didn't get a thing done yesterday."

Unbroken is the life story of Louie Zemperini, the Olympic runner and World War II hero. Zemperini became a Christian inspirational speaker later in life after going to a Billy Graham revival.

"That's a pretty amazing story. Have you gotten to the Billy Graham part yet?" I already know that Geoff is not religious and doesn't go to any church. Still I'm a little surprised by his response.

He huffs. "No, but when I get to that part, that's when I'll throw it away. I'm done with it. People like Billy Graham should be . . ." He stops himself, but not before his dismissal is duly noted. Geoff is a curious, intelligent man, and the wilderness provides lots of time for a guy to be alone with his thoughts. Maybe that's where he came up with his philosophy of life. One thing is for certain: religion sure doesn't float his boat.

Some guys get defensive at the mere mention of faith. Many have been poisoned by a bad experience in their past. To make sure it never happens again, they will have nothing to do with organized religion. I don't know if anything like that had happened to Geoff. As for me, I'm not too disgusted to talk about religion. I'm just chicken. I can offend people by talking about pretty much anything else without giving it a second thought. There's something different about religion, though. Religion feels serious. You shouldn't talk to a guy about it until you're both ready.

I've bonked my head so many times that I've taken to wearing a baseball cap even when I'm indoors. I usually turn it backwards so it doesn't cut down on my field of vision. I still bonk my head, but with the hat it bleeds less. When Geoff shows up for his next visit, as soon as I open the front door, he says, "Who was the first guy to wear his ball cap backwards on TV?" Geoff is no slouch when it comes to trivia.

I scratch my stubbly chin. "Let's see. Gomer Pyle wore his marine cap sort of cockeyed. Gilligan wore a bucket hat.

And I don't know what cousin Goober had on his head. All right, Geoff, I give up."

"It was Oscar Madison from *The Odd Couple*. You know, the sportswriter. Kind of a slob."

Geoff knows I'm a wannabe writer. He's had to poke around both my writing cave and my reading cave, trying to get to the baseboards. The implication here is more than subliminal. I consider it a compliment. The piles in the Rube's caves are organized messes.

"I've been meaning to ask you, Geoff, do you have a nickname?"

Geoff does. By his hesitation and then a slightly pained expression, I get the feeling that if he had his way, he'd never tell anyone about it.

He was on one of his backpacking trips with a couple of guys, sitting around the campfire after a long day. The night was calm until a rogue gust of wind caused the fire to flare up. Geoff was the only guy sitting downwind. He barely escaped by quickly scooting backwards on all fours, like a scalded lobster with his butt never quite getting off the ground. After that, his buddies call him Scootch.

I have a wide smile. "That's a cool nickname. I can work with that."

Geoff grimaces like he regrets it already.

I'm quick to assure him, "No worries, Geoff. Your secret is good with me."

I tap the half dome and lie again. "Stays right here."

Geoff hikes a lot of miles in places where not many others go. I'm not sure I could hike with Geoff. I may not be man enough. Geoff is not just a maverick; he's a lone wolf.

Not long ago, he was hiking another remote tract when he came upon an old iron gate standing by itself. There wasn't a fence post, a fence rail, or a roll of wire in sight. Just a single gate from a bygone era, no longer connected to anything. Geoff had worked this land as a cowboy and cattle drover many years ago when the area was dotted with cattle ranches. He's explored many unofficial routes that don't show up on any maps. Nobody knows the Cave Creek wilderness as well as he does. Not even the mapmakers.

Upon examining the gate further, he realized that he had actually built that gate as a ranch hand. He had dug the footings and installed it himself over thirty years ago. The fencing is all gone, and the gate serves no purpose now. But it's standing straight and square and still working. Ready and able to do the job. I can hear the satisfaction in his voice and see the pride in his face. The latch and strike still line up and shut with a sure and solid metal *ka-chunk*, like a round being chambered into a Mossberg 500. Locked and loaded. Ready to go. That gate was built to last by a guy who takes pride in his work. Geoff's voice trails off, letting me provide my own ending to his story.

The story of Geoff's gate gets me thinking how a good man is a lot like a good gate. Strong. Durable. Functional. Able to withstand the elements. Able to guard against enemy intruders. Able to show the way to the narrow path.

I'm excited. "Geoff, I have an idea. Listen up."

"Uh oh," is his terse reply.

"Since you are like a desert father in these parts, you should pick your favorite route, build the path, and then offer it to the hiking world as an official trail. They would likely name it after you. The Scootch Trail. Wouldn't that be cool?"

Geoff is unmoved.

I up the ante. "I'll help you build it out."

Geoff grins. "That's more of a reason not to do it."

I didn't help my case, but I'm not giving up.

"They would mark it with your special gate, and a sign above it: *The Scootch Trail. Abandon all pretense ye who enter here.* Think about it, Geoff. Your name on an official map. The legend of Scootch would be etched in the annals of Arizona folklore. You'd be right up there with George Hayduke and the Lost Dutchman."

Geoff is really a humble guy, and now he's starting to squirm. The Rube is getting precariously close to the proverbial line.

I let him off the hook. "I'm only half-kidding, Geoff. But seriously, have you thought about what your legacy will be when you're gone?"

His reply comes so quick it seems like he's not only thought about it, he's already made up his mind. As he heads through the side gate to the back yard, Geoff shoots back over his shoulder. "Naaah. Don't want one. Legacies are made to be forgotten."

For Geoff, legacies must be like religion. They're not worth contemplating. For the present, there are too many places yet to go, and too much yet to do—more important things. And never enough daylight. Yeah, Geoff is a rare bird, different from the typical guy in so many ways. And yet, as unique as he is, he's just like the rest of us.

Searching.

INTERLUDE: ALL MANNER OF MEN

Whether we like it or not, we men need each other. Being in fellowship with other men is not just something to do when, or if, it's convenient. Fellowship is not optional. God could save the world by himself. His plan of salvation doesn't need to include the cooperation of men. Rather, he chooses to implement his plan through his Son and his ongoing relationship with his creatures.

A life of heroic virtue is not just about you. It's also not just about you and God. It's about you, God, and a bunch of other self-centered, annoying, obnoxious, cowardly, and lazy men who are occasionally selfless and virtuous. If you don't recognize yourself in that litany, you can add arrogant and prideful to the list. Our mission is to help each other become great souls in the eyes of God. The Lord uses all manner of men, even the worst of sinners, to accomplish his will and bring about good.

It should be unsettling to think that how I respond to the next guy I encounter has some effect on my own eternal destiny. What if he's a haughty blowhard with an opposing worldview? What if he wears a perpetually smug expression with a condescending attitude? What if he looks different and speaks with a funny accent? If the goal of our actions is to arrive at love, I have much growing to do.

Scripture recounts only one noteworthy thing Jesus did for the first thirty years of his life. He got lost for three days. If the greatest man who ever lived was a slow starter, there's certainly still hope for us. For thirty years he faithfully prepared for his mission. He dedicated himself to prayer and the study of the scriptures. He was obedient to the will of his heavenly Father and the authority of his earthly father. He honored Joseph and Mary and grew in virtue and wisdom. Hardy epic stuff by earthly standards. But at the appointed time, Jesus would do the really hard things.

Here we are two millennia later, and each of us has been given a mission too. You may not think your mission is monumental or world-changing, but if you fulfill it faithfully, it will be life-changing for you and those whose lives intersect with yours.

We're not promised a red carpet or a primrose lane, but we have been given a map, a map describing a narrow path. When you choose to bypass the wide, easy road and enter through the narrow gate, your epic journey begins. Following the path to the pinnacle is the adventure of a heroic life.

Do me a favor, will you? Every so often, drop a few breadcrumbs for the Rube.

DAY TRIPPERS AND
FIRST TIMERS

I t's easy to gather some guys to have a few beers and watch their favorite team. Just for fun, try getting them to pursue faith with the same enthusiasm. Prepare to be underwhelmed. It boils down to a guy's comfort with the familiar and his fear of the unknown. It's the same principle that can make the Boys' Trip a tough sale to a new guy.

A four-day trip with the Rube takes a leap of faith over a gulf too wide for the typical guy. This is where the day trip gets off the bench. A half-day outing is less threatening. Throw in the beers and a promise to have him home before dark, and a first-timer might nibble on that one. We're not shooting for a change in destiny here. Not yet.

It's a sweltering day in the valley when the siren song of the high-country interrupts another of the Rube's daydreams. Four Peaks is howling again. The boys haven't been out of their cages for a while, so it's time to float the idea of a mid-summer day trip. I troll the men's study groups and get two bites, Big Wayne, a Boys' Trip veteran, and Rex, a first-timer.

Rex is about the last guy I'd expect to be a hiker. He doesn't strike me as the outdoorsy type. Nobody I know has hiked with Rex. That could well be because he's never hiked before. That would make this his maiden voyage. We'll have to be gentle on him. Hiking with a new guy is always a crapshoot, but this one could be especially dicey.

Meeting at my place at 5:45 a.m., Rex arrives looking like he's going on safari. Big Wayne and I are wearing shorts and wicking t-shirts. Rex is sporting freshly pressed khaki pants, a crisp, long-sleeve denim shirt, a fishing vest, and a wide-brimmed bush hat. His shoes appear to be Hush Puppies. A canvas book bag from the St. Vincent DePaul Thrift Store is slung over his shoulder. He looks like a mash-up of Marlon Perkins and The Man with the Yellow Hat.

With so many easy targets, I can't resist a good-natured jab. "Hey, Rex, what's with the big game hat and the bag?" I joke. "You bringing your pet monkey in that knapsack?"

Rex has a comeback for everything, but this time he's speechless. His trademark grin says, "Not bad, Rube, but I'll get you back for that one."

I'm trying to avoid disrespecting an elder, but I'm not trying all that hard. "Rex, the park ranger look is cool and everything, but do you have anything a little less, er, formal? You don't want to overheat or blow a gasket in the middle of nowhere. Rescues are expensive on the mountain." I will come to learn that offending Rex will take a crack much worse than that.

He mutters, "I'm good. I've got AAA. They cover jump starts and towing."

Rex pulls a contraption from his pocket and points it at the driveway.

"Whoa, is that Steve Zodiac's ray gun? You're a *Fireball XL-5* fan, too!"

"Nope. Temperature gun. Let me worry about the heat, Rube."

Rex pulls the trigger and glances at the screen. "Sixty degrees. I'll tell you when it gets hot." Yep. This is going to be a trip.

Big Wayne is a tall, sturdy type who played open division basketball after college. Wayne was better known as a street fighter, so naturally he was the team enforcer. Take a note, Rube. When it's time to choose up, you want to be on Big Wayne's team.

As a hiker, Wayne's a grinder. He won't abide anyone waiting on him. While the other guys hike ahead, Wayne plows onward at his own pace, slow and steady. What he lacks in speed he makes up for in drive. I've learned not to worry much about Wayne hiking solo from behind. In a square off of man versus bear, Big Wayne would be at least even money.

Rex is not athletic and by his own admission not a hiker. He started coming to men's study group a couple years back, and tales of past junkets have sparked his curiosity. For reasons known only to him, Rex must think the Boys' Trip is something he needs to check out in person. A leading-edge baby boomer, his most agile assets are a keen mind and a quick wit. Years of shrewd observation have honed them to a razor's edge. Rex sees humor in practically everything, especially the irony under the surface and between the lines. Chat with Rex, and you best be on your toes and ready for a spontaneous outburst of hearty laughter. He can be even more of an instigator than the Rube. But his provocation is productive and purposeful, intended to stimulate thoughtful discussion. The Rube agitates others sometimes just for the pure heck of it.

The hike from Lone Pine to Brown's Saddle is pleasant if not a little warm. We start out at 8:05 a.m., and it's exactly 82°F. Rex's digital temperature gun is a recurring source of amusement. Give him any kind of a gun, and a boy is easily entertained.

On the edge of the trail, a Mojave rattler curls up under a granite ledge. Rex crouches like he's about to crawl in after it.

"Don't get too close, Rex. Rattlers can strike distances up to their body length."

"They say snakes are cold blooded. I want to see what the gun says."

Rex challenges conventional wisdom on everything. Once he's tested it and found it steadfast, then he becomes a firm proponent, but not a moment before. He makes a guy think about stuff on a different level. It can be exhausting.

Rex zeroes in on a scat pile on the trail. "Hey, Rube, how fresh is poop when it's between seventy-six and eighty-seven degrees?"

"Crikey, that's a pretty big range, Rex. What gives?"

Rex cycles his gun off and back on again. "The critter made two separate deposits, maybe. Could be his cell phone went off in the middle of his business. That's why I leave mine in the car."

It would be fun to give Rex a little of his own business. I scratch my chin. In Dan'l Boone mode, I drawl, "We got black bears in these parts. This here looks like fresh bear scat. It's got black berries in it."

Rex's not buying it. He quips, "That doesn't mean anything. I like blackberries."

I take a knee to get a closer look. Rex cracks, "Sheez, Rube, you need to genuflect to it?"

I'm not giving up. "My guess is black bear, a pretty big one, ten minutes ahead."

Rex suspects I'm full of the same stuff piled on the trail. He mutters, "If you're right, Rube, we're gonna need a different type of gun." He starts rustling through his book bag. Wayne mops his brow and gives me a look like we're better off not knowing what other surprises he's got in that bag.

Rex looks up from his rummaging. "Hey, Rube, do bears eat monkey?"

The official trail ends at Brown's Saddle where the views are impressive. I expect Rex will be happy to hang back and poke around the ridge top while Big Wayne and I make the summit scramble to Brown's Peak. Big Wayne has a different plan. After an up-close look at the gnarly 800-foot-tall scree chute, he's convinced. "I'm not going up there. I'm not good with heights." Wayne sweats a lot as it is, but he's dripping now. The irony doesn't escape me.

In his hoop days, Big Wayne played above the rim. He could throw the rock down with two hands behind his head. He had some serious hops. To admit being nervous about a high place with no guardrails is the right play of a virtue card. Better to humble yourself than to risk injury.

I try to be reassuring. "Don't sweat it, Wayne. My last time up here, the grownups wouldn't go near the chute. Only the kid would go." The two men were both well-conditioned and athletic, but the geeky teenager was the only one fearless. I was more surprised his dad trusted me to take him up there. It's not like he had a son to spare.

With Big Wayne out of the running, I have no expectations Rex will go anywhere near the chute. I turn to the Swede who is looking very flushed at the moment. "Rex, we can hike around to the Amethyst Mine from here. No worries. I don't need to do the summit."

Rex wipes his brow with his sleeve and takes a swig from a water bottle. He appears unmoved, almost bored. "Whatever," he replies. "We came to do the mountain. Let's go on up, and I'll let you know when I've had enough."

I'm not convinced Rex is all in. "Are you sure?"

Wrong move, Rube. Now he's borderline miffed.

Rex glares and snaps, "I said, let's go on up. Am I speaking Laplander?"

The spittle flying is my clue that he's serious. From here on I better be looking over my shoulder. He may have his Swedish battle-ax in that bag.

If I were a better trip leader, I would put my foot down and say that's enough for a first hike. The gnarly climb is too much for him. I should say, "No way, Rex. You can't do that." But I've raised his ire already and don't want to risk it again.

I point out the Amethyst Trail to Big Wayne, and he sets off down the ridge toward the trail junction. Rex and I start working our way around to the base of the ravine. Even in midsummer the summit tower overshadows the chute, so it's a cool 62°F.

I feel the need to make up to Rex now. "I've got to give it to you, Rex, that temperature gun is sure handy. Thrift store special?"

He replies, "Nope. Cereal box." This guy never misses.

When we reach ground zero for the climb, I pull a pair of gloves from the top pocket and stow my pack behind a shrub. I motion to Rex. "Now would be the time to get your gloves out, Rex. You're going to be using your hands from here on."

Rex fishes around in his knapsack, producing a pair of large quilted gardening mitts. "I wondered why you told me to bring these things."

The mitts complete the look. There's nobody up here to impress but, even if there were, Rex wouldn't change a thing.

Rube, the hike leader, is not done coaching yet. "I'll go first, Rex, if that's OK, to show you the best route. In a steep ravine, you want to give the guy above you plenty of room. If he kicks a rock loose, you need time to get out of the way."

Rex shrugs. "It's not a race."

I'm not a fast climber as it is, but if I want to keep an eye on Rex, I'll need to find an even lower gear. It's clear he doesn't want or need any advice from the Rube. I'll give him his space and check on him every fifty to a hundred feet. Each time I pause to peer back down the gully, I expect to see Rex sitting on a boulder with a library book. His pet monkey will be chattering away on his lap, pointing and turning the pages. And that will be the end of that. Instead, Rex keeps climbing higher, slowly and steadily.

After forty minutes of this stop-and-go, I figure I better wait up for Rex before the final pitch. I want to see his reaction when he sets foot on the roof. I've been on Brown's Peak when the summit rocks and shrubs were coated in ladybugs thick as lingonberry jam on a crumpet. But that was a cool fall day. Today it's a sizzling 99°F on the mountain, and there's not a smart ladybug in sight. Instead, Brown's Peak is Woodstock for black gnats. This mob is not seeking peace and love, but our imminent demise.

Within seconds of summiting, Rex and I resemble the Woolly Willy brothers. We're spinning and swatting, spitting and snorting gnats from every exposed orifice. Hundreds of tiny kamikazes cover my white shirt like ground pepper. Rex manages to snap a couple of photos before we're forced to flee the scene.

I'm bummed Rex was unable to enjoy the views or bask in his rookie achievement. It would have been fun to hear him expound from such a lofty perch. Where he was a tad agitated with the Rube before the climb, this situation with the gnats doesn't bother him in the least. What makes him so unflappable?

The post hike fellowship is as much a part of the adventure as the hike. The closest town to Four Peaks is little more than a speed bump, but it has its own purveyor of offbeat color, the Punkin Center Lodge Bar and Grill. Rex loves the quirky backwaters, and this place suits him like a Goodwill sports coat.

Rex, Wayne, and I slide our stools up to the bar. The Rube has a couple of strikes left and decides to go down swinging. "To tell you the truth, Rex, I didn't think you'd be much of a hiker. You surprised me up there, pal."

Rex grins. "Raiding, burning, and pillaging keeps a guy in shape. That stuff's not easy. It's the Viking in my blood." He signals the barkeep with three fingers. The twinkle in his eye gives him away.

Taking comes naturally to men, but giving is difficult. Rex makes it look easy. He is generous in sharing the fruits of his hard-earned wisdom, and quick to speak his mind without a guy having to ask. He carries a shopping bag or a satchel everywhere he goes, and it never lacks a thoughtful gift for someone. He loves surprising people with a thrift store treasure or a book scavenged just for them.

He's also an avid promoter of truth. Lest anyone think Four Peaks wasn't really a challenge for him, Rex provides an email update a few days after the hike. "Recovery- Day Three" reads like a geezer's medical chart: "Thigh muscles still painfully sore. Still can't do a deep knee bend, or a shallow one either. Hard to even sit down or get up. Blisters are mostly gone, though. First day without painkillers." And the best line is: "Let me preface these remarks by saying I was pleased with the hike on Sunday. Thanks."

Yeah, Rex is a defender of truth even when it hurts.

The day trip is intended to be an appetizer to break in a first timer, but Rex's maiden voyage has been a veritable feast. I can't help but think I'm witnessing the dawn of a Boys' Trip legend.

INTERLUDE: YOU CAN'T DO THAT

The Boys' Trip is training for the challenges a guy might face in the real world back home. That's not just a sales pitch to convince a wary spouse. As sons, brothers, husbands, fathers, and grandfathers, our mission is to protect and defend, serve and provide. To be ready for whatever comes against us and our families. We may not get a second chance.

Every trip includes a trek requiring a reasonable level of fitness. I tell the guys they get one shot. No do-overs, no mulligans. Strength and conditioning are helpful, but endurance and a tolerance for pain are essential. The Rube's back-of-the-envelope trip planning requires a guy to display more patience and grace than he should have to. Again, good practice.

I look for an opportunity to stretch our boundaries on purpose to give the guys a chance to prove something to themselves. Or to disprove a doubter. We're building our fighting spirits here. A hike qualifies as a worthy test if at any point in the planning process a valid authority figure declares, "You guys can't do that."

That kind of direct challenge appeals to the scrapper in me. My record as a fighter is suspect, but if I want something bad enough, I can be persistent. If any part of my character resembles tenacity or determination, it's less likely from a wellspring of virtue than it is my hard-headed stubborn streak.

Even a hint of disdain or superiority from another guy raises the Rube's hackles. Up on Four Peaks, Rex showed the same fire. A man takes umbrage when he senses a challenge to his manhood. It's a scary thought that Rex might be like me. Without adult supervision, we make a dangerous duo.

On the trail, the latest tech apparel and greatest gear don't count as much as grit and determination. Rex would have climbed that hill wearing flip-flops, a toga, and a little crown of oak leaves. Short or tall, large or lean, physical characteristics matter less than the size of a guy's heart. Every man has innate heroic virtue because of whose image he bears. For some guys, the slumbering bear seems a more fitting image. Striving to achieve a goal believed to be out of his reach might help awaken a guy's noble qualities from hibernation.

The experience of adventure helps him be more prepared when his number is drawn. But it doesn't include a risk-free trial or money back guarantee. His testing will likely occur when he least expects it. None of us knows the day or the hour.

The place he comes under heaviest fire might be in the heart of the wilderness. His battle might be most intense in his own living room. He could be at the peak of his physical prowess or he might be over the hill. Wherever he is, before he's faced with the test of his life, a guy needs to look in the mirror and consider three questions.

Do I buckle under pressure, when the world sneers with contempt, "Who do you think you are?"

Do I fall back into my safe, comfortable routine when the voice of doubt whispers, "You don't belong here?"

Do I sound the retreat when the voice of fear says, "You can't do that"?

ARE YOU EXPERIENCED?

"**G**ood morning. We're here to kayak the Colorado River." I lead the boys into the shop like I'm the reincarnation of John Wesley Powell.

Terry, the shop proprietor, responds from behind the counter.

"Good morning, men. Brittany left a note saying you guys want four kayaks instead of a raft?" Looking up from her paperwork, she peers at us over the top of her glasses. "Are you experienced?"

It seems like a harmless question.

We arrived in Moab, Utah, late yesterday afternoon. While the boys scoped out the town, I scurried into the adventure travel shop, barely beating the turn of the "Sorry. We're Closed" sign.

Brittany was working the desk, and tried to sell me on taking a single raft for our group of four. But I would have no part of it. A raft is great when you're doing a whitewater river, and you need a guide. But this run is supposed to be a wide, moderate float. A raft would be too soft. We're better than that.

The last thing these guys need is a day lollygagging in a cushy raft while a guide does all the work. This is a Boys' Trip. We're looking for a man-against-the-river adventure. We're here to work. We'll take the kayaks. A river trip in a single kayak is a different animal. It's all on you. If anything goes wrong, there's no one to blame but yourself—and the guy who set up the trip.

Terry's question isn't confrontational, yet I feel compelled to turn to Chad. He's the guy in our party with the credit card. "You're up, Doctor." Since he's paying the bill, Chad is theoretically the responsible party.

To Terry's question, he replies truthfully, "Yes."

Chad is a proficient paddler, so his experience will need to be wide enough to throw a safety net over our entire party. As for the rest of us, Roger knows enough to be dangerous; the Rube is not nearly as good as I think I am, and I'd be surprised if Rex knows which side of the kayak is up. Terry didn't specify what kind of experience.

With experienced paddlers, Terry gets a break because she can give the abbreviated version of the safety briefing. We gather around the counter. "Be sure to wear your PFD at all times," she tells us. Rex appears puzzled. He heard BFD and probably wonders why she's using salty language already. She barely knows us.

I'm trying not to sound like a wise guy, but I can't believe there's not more. I have to say something. I pipe up, "Is that it for the briefing?"

Terry replies, "No, there's also this." She hands Chad a clipboard. "You each need to provide your ID info and read and sign the risk form."

Professional adventure companies are in the business of managing risk, especially their own. That's why everyone must sign his life away before being allowed on one of their trips. The Acknowledgment of Risk form is standard fare for a trip like this. Among other items, it states: "A river trip entails unavoidable risks including the usual blah, blah, blah, . . . and death. The undersigned takes full responsibility for knowing the risks involved." Sign and date below. Now the safety briefing is done.

Terry must sense my hesitancy, so she turns to me and says, "There's only one spot on this stretch of the Colorado where you can get into real trouble, and that's at Red Cliffs. But experienced paddlers will have no problems."

Terry doesn't know whom she's dealing with here. The Rube can get into trouble before his feet hit the floor in the morning.

She hands me a map of the Colorado River north of Moab. "Follow me out front, and I'll get you guys set up," she says as she heads for the door.

We plan to kayak eleven river miles and, perusing the map, I count seven named rapids in that section. I've seen some crazy names for rapids before, but none of these sounds too bad. Except the one called Trash Compactor. It's the final rapid before our take-out beach, so, heck, we can swim to the beach if we wipe out there. This is going to be awesome.

I'm trying to sound like a seasoned boater as I lead the boys outside. "Hey, Terry. How is it flowing right now?"

"It's 4,350 CFS, which is low as the Colorado goes. But trust me, you're going to get wet. There's no getting around that."

Without a point of reference, the flow number means nothing to me, but the getting wet part is what I like to hear.

Out in front of the shop, Terry stops at the trailer with the boats already loaded on it. The kayaks are impressive, rigid, and durable, fit gear for pros like us.

"The inflatables are self-bailing, so you couldn't sink one if you tried," she chuckles. "They're so stable, you won't be doing any Eskimo rolls in one of these."

I wink at Rex and think that's good because we wouldn't know an Eskimo roll from an Eskimo pie.

Terry points to a rack with equipment hanging from it. "Everybody grab a PFD and try it on. You want it really tight."

By now, Rex has figured out that PFD means personal flotation device. He's a quick study.

Next, Terry demonstrates the procedure for deflating the inflatable kayaks. "Don't do this until *after* you're all done and up on the beach." Her emphasis implies that some idiot must have deflated his kayak when he was still on the river. I'll bet that guy wasn't experienced. Anyhow, it's nice to know the Rube won't be the first.

Terry mentions again the one spot for us to be especially wary. "Lower flows like today make certain rapids worse than they are at high flows. Red Cliffs is one of those. Just stay left of the big pour-over."

I'm scribbling notes on my map. "Wait, I don't see that on here. Where exactly is it; how will we recognize it?"

Terry rolls her eyes. "Oh, you'll know it when you see it. If you fall asleep on that one, you're going to get intimate with the river real fast."

The three stooges nudge each other and snicker. Getting intimate. That's a good one. She's probably just trying to talk like one of the boys. You know, trying to spice things up a little for us. Terry is pretty cool.

The map has printed notes at each set of rapids to direct the novice kayaker away from trouble. That's more than we need. After all, we're experienced.

The Colorado River has carved out a remarkable thirty-mile section of northeastern Utah north of Moab. Our shuttle driver says Utah State Highway 128, which parallels the river, has been named the second most scenic highway in America by *National Geographic* behind only Highway One in California. We're at the tail end of rafting season in the west when river flows are at their lowest. Even if it's a bit slow, this stretch will be memorable just for the scenery.

After an hour's ride, our driver drops us off twenty miles upriver where we put the kayaks in at Onion Creek at 10:30 a.m. I undo the top buckle of my PFD and tuck the map into my shirt pocket. After a recent rain the Colorado is the color of a latte. At 62°, it's a brisk, very cool latte.

The class rating of rapids and rivers is a subjective exercise. The rating varies based on the time of year, the CFS flow, and any new obstructions resulting from runoff or rockslides. The International Scale of River Difficulty goes from class I to class VI. By the book, this stretch of the Colorado is class I with several scattered class II rapids. A novice kayaker can't know where he stands or sits on the scale until he's actually tested in real life. He can just venture a guess based on past experience. I figure I'm somewhere between class II and III. But I could be wrong.

The map doesn't have any notes on the first two rapids, so we're on our own. The first ones come up shortly after put-in. I hang back and let Chad lead Roger and Rex through the best line. The river is moving at a lively pace, and the rapids are enough to keep my attention. Everybody seems to be having a good time. Rex is not commenting one way or the other.

As we approach the third set of rapids, my PFD is making it tough to get the map out of my pocket, so I undo another buckle. It's starting to warm up, so it feels good to loosen things up a bit.

The note for the next rapid, Cloudburst, says to stay just left of the top-center hole where two large rocks appear at low flows. Interesting. "Hole" is a word I've never associated with a river. The low rumble of larger waves is growing in intensity as we near the rapid. This one is bigger than the others. My voice is nearly drowned out as I holler from behind, "Stay left! Stay left!" Chad already has the route lined out and sails through in front of a seventy-foot wall of rock. The three of us follow Chad's line. Hey, we aren't bad. I'm having such a grand time I forget to look for the alleged hole.

On the next set, the map calls for a center run and cautions to watch for rocks and holes at low flows. "Center! Center!" I shout above the rush of the river. The rattle and roll sends a couple of water cannon shots over my bow. The chilly water feels great. After sailing through with glee, I'm beginning to trust this system. Maybe we are pretty good. I still haven't seen anything I would call a hole.

Next up is a relatively long stretch of smooth water. A group of rafters just put in about a half mile in front of us, and they're making such a ruckus their cackling echoes off the red cliffs. Tourists. Rafting seems more of a party than a serious adventure. Kayaking is where the real men hang out. We would be better to relax and put some distance between us and them.

I'm feeling pretty good right now. So far, there's no sign of the Colorado's notorious afternoon head winds, winds so bad that river guides here won't speak the W-word for fear of jinxing their trip. Instead they use the code name, Mister Gusty. These guys are so superstitious. Mister G must be taking the day off because the weather is darn near perfect.

We let the party boats get ahead a bit before we start paddling again. There's over a two-mile stretch where the river is calm. The red rock formations are mesmerizing, including familiar icons like Fisher Towers, the Professor and Students, and the Priest and Nuns. The La Sal Mountains with their frosting of early snow provide a backdrop worthy of a postcard. We'll be hiking up on those peaks tomorrow if things go according to plan.

After twenty minutes of idyllic drifting, the rumble of approaching rapids rustles me from my daydreaming. Just ahead, the river narrows and makes a sharp right turn, followed by a quick left. I'm quite a way behind the boys, but if they follow Chad's line, they'll be all right.

I forgot, what's the name of that rapid with the big pour-over Terry was talking about? I pull the map from my shirt pocket. The next one is White's Rapid. That name doesn't ring a bell. The notes say to watch for huge waves and holes center right. I really don't like that word huge. Then it says, "Stay left at top, back to center or center left." Now I'm confused. This could be the place, but where is the pour-over? Is it left, right, or center? The boys are now already around the bend and out of sight.

I'm fiddling with the map, paddle in my lap, when a mighty current jerks the boat to the center of the channel. I drop the map, grab my paddle, and my brain is screaming, "Left! Left!" I bury my left paddle straining too late and too weak against a hydraulic beast I'm no match for.

A split-second later, I meet Mister H. My boat drops out from under me and plunges into space. Everything is airborne: map, hat, paddle, and my stomach. When I smack down, my half-buckled PFD is up over my head. With pour-over water pounding me under, I save my vest by my fingernails. I'm sputtering for air, hanging on with both hands, and kicking frantically toward the light. The instant I break the surface, my kayak bounces, flips, and lands upside down on top of me.

Now, it's dark as night, and I'm racing through rapids backwards, my head bouncing like a pinball off the sides of a stiff rubber casket. I manage to flip the boat over and thrash about until I'm going with the flow. I hoist myself up on the sidewall and try to point my feet downstream, but I'm dancing with a stubborn partner who won't give up the lead. My left ankle glances off a boulder. I skim over submerged rocks, buffeted like britches in a wash cycle. Working frantically to keep my toes up and out in front, I'm terrified of getting a foot or a leg stuck in a rock jam.

I'm a hapless hitchhiker clinging to a baby beluga, and we're headed straight for a frothing beast at twelve o'clock. The center channel is over thirty feet deep, so the top of this rock jamb is taller than a three-story building. Hurtling toward the curl of white spray, I tuck my knees up and tap-dance over the top, not knowing what's on the other side. Hope it's not Mister Hole's angry cousin.

When I splash down into smooth water, I can finally breathe again. The curtain falls after my turn on *Dancing with the Stars*. Where's the applause? There is just exhaustion, relief and, oh yeah, gratitude. Everything was happening so fast and furiously. I was too busy scratching for my life to give God even a thought, much less a prayer. Though I forgot him, he didn't abandon me.

Fortunately, the boys don't forget me either. I hope they didn't see anything. I should tell them I'm being the sweeper like the last hiker in a group who makes sure no stragglers are left behind. I've been trolling underwater for bodies. Has anyone seen Rex?

Chad and Roger paddle back upstream to assess the damage. Roger is first on the scene. I must look pretty wrung out because he seems genuinely worried.

"Are you OK? What are you doing in the water?"

Stuck to the sidewall of my kayak, I don't have the energy to fake it. I have to catch my breath before wheezing a weak reply. "Do I look OK to you?" I'm sucking gas. "How's my hair?"

"Lost at sea." Roger is never wanting for a wisecrack. "Did you save the pancake puppies?" Sometimes he can be too much.

"Do you suppose that was the spot Terry was talking about?" Roger asks meekly.

I have just about had it. "Ya think?" I wheeze.

The official story should be that I got in the water only because I had to pee. But that would stretch my already thin credibility beyond breaking. Besides, they may have seen too much. Speaking of relief, however, now is as good a chance as I'm gonna get.

When I let go of the kayak, my fingers are cramped like rooster claws, and my forearms are twitching from fatigue. I'm hanging limply from my loose PFD, my nose barely above water, when my Tilly hat appears. Then my paddle. They float up to Roger's boat, like, "Have you seen our skipper? He was right here a second ago, and then, *whoosh*." That Tilly is an expensive hat; a gift from Vickie designed to protect my brain from frying. It appears to have failed. The only permanent loss is the map. My pride appears to have survived intact.

Chad paddles up and is way more amused than concerned. He says he saw everything from downstream. Great. He nearly rolled his boat laughing at my hijinks. It must have been pretty amusing, maybe like the opening sequence from the campy Saturday morning TV series, *Land of the Lost*. Immortal. If that image doesn't work for you, just picture the Tidy Bowl Man a split second after the flush. Every old guy remembers him.

The boys could make all sorts of "getting intimate with the river" cracks right now, but to their credit they have mercy on me. They'll have the rest of the trip to get their shots in. I can hear them now, wailing away to the Credence Clearwater tune Proud Bruber, "Rollin' on the River." Next up, will be the Blues Brothers' "Hole Man." It's going to be a long drive home.

Chad is still chuckling when he reports, "Sorry to break this to you, Captain, but there are more waves just ahead. You need to get back in your boat."

We need to get going again for Rex's sake, too. I'm sure a landlubber like him is antsy to be done. He's ready to feel solid ground beneath his feet again.

The boys form a two-boat convoy, and corral my kayak. Chad extends his paddle, and I grab the blade and pull myself out of the water. I flop like a hooked flounder across my boat for a few seconds before sliding into the seat. I buckle my PFD all the way up and cinch it tight. Thanks for the advice, Terry.

It's good that I'm tossed right back into the fray. My cowboy pal Willy says when you get thrown from a horse, you need to get right back on him. Show him who's boss. I had become complacent and overconfident on the first half of the trip. I was due for a correction, and there's nothing like a good licking to refocus a wayward boy's attention.

Coming into the next rapid, I'm more anxious than excited. But I'm fully engaged. I'm no longer snoozing in Margaritaville. The last half of the trip is a different kind of good. It's more challenging to run the rapids without advance information from a map. It forces me to focus on getting through what I'm in at the moment rather than worry about what's coming up. What's ahead will be upon me soon enough. I'll deal with it then. Sort of like life. It's possible to have too much information. A rapid is what it is. It doesn't become bigger and badder after somebody names it Trash Compactor. Only men are capable of changing character to live up or down to a reputation.

A few days after returning from the Boys' Trip to Moab, Rex walks into Men's Group with a paper grocery bag. "I got something for you, Jay." He hands me the bag.

Rex is our authority on slang and ethnic slurs. He says Jay means Rube in Kansas-speak. Inside the bag is a book with a plastic protective cover, a how-to guide to whitewater kayaking.

I'm touched. "Wow, this looks like an expensive book. This is for me, Rex?"

He deadpans, "I'm never kayaking again, so you might as well have it. And it was expensive, a buck at the thrift store. It was senior day, though, so seventy-five cents."

"You shouldn't have, Rex. I don't deserve this."

"Yeah, you do, Jay. It's waterproof." Then he adds with a grin, "There's some stuff in there that would have been good to know before getting intimate. Maybe it'll help you next time."

Rex didn't have the time of his life kayaking. He forgot to put sunscreen on his legs, so after our day on the river, he was sporting some pretty hot drumsticks. On the drive home, his legs were so sore, he couldn't put his usual khakis on. He looked like he was wearing the old-style Cincinnati Redlegs' baseball pants with the knee high red stirrups. Ouch.

I'm not too worried about Rex, though. He's a Swede so he's practically a Viking. Sailing is in his blood. He'll get on the water again.

Reading up on holes in Rex's whitewater guide, I realize I got off lucky. These things are the demons of the river, to be avoided by paddlers like bad clichés by a writer. The last word is advice I could have seen coming a mile away, yet I still managed to miss it. The best way to handle a hole is to avoid it in the first place. But that's not the whole truth.

If a guy is far from God, it's easy to forget about him when all hell is breaking loose. It's natural for a worldly man to think about everything but God precisely when he needs him the most. Like me, many guys still have far to go in our quest for virtue because that should frighten us a lot more than it does.

INTERLUDE: THE WHOLE TRUTH

Modern Western culture is becoming indifferent to faith. Many places seem downright hostile to religion. A man actively living his faith might feel like he's navigating a turbulent river. If a religion such as Catholicism is faithful to its doctrine and tradition, it will be at cross currents with the liberal social stream. Religion should be a corrective to a permissive, anything goes lifestyle, so a guy is rightly concerned if his faith is never at odds with the world. It's not likely that the world is the one making concessions.

Holes are all around us. Temptations are disguised as good things, and dangers don't announce themselves in advance. If a guy goes to sleep at the paddle, the current will take him into the nearest hole. The Church can help him steer clear of the holes, but he must put in the work to be ready. If he were living his faith all the time, he wouldn't be scrambling to put it on when a crisis strikes. But still, trips and falls are inevitable.

The point of any adventure is to emerge with more wisdom, not for stockpiling, but for investing in others. The people who need us the most are not likely to come looking for us, so we need to go where they are. That will put us closer to the danger where we risk being drawn into it. We survive the falls by the grace of God. With the guidance of the Church and the help of our brothers, we get back in the boat and make another run at it. Hopefully, we're smarter and stronger from the experience.

EMIGRANT PEAK, RECALCULATING

The destination for Boys' Trip 2013 is Yellowstone, but the government shutdown has closed the National Parks two days before our arrival. Good timing.

You'd think that the closing of a trophy destination so close to the launch date would throw a trip into turmoil. Not so, pilgrim. With the Rube, turmoil is a normal state of affairs.

For our base of operations, the Hobbit reserved a cabin near Gardiner, a quaint town that bumps up against the north entrance to Yellowstone. The boys and I fly into Bozeman, where Hobbit and his twenty-year-old son, Sam, pick us up for the two-hour drive south to Gardiner. Hobbit rented a white Ford panel van for the occasion. This ancient rig is the classic youth group vehicle, the type used to shuttle teens to retreats or service activities. It's a nice touch since we're on a mission of sorts. Not exactly a Blues Brothers' reclamation project, but a mission from God, nonetheless.

Sam can only be with us for one day, so our flagship hike needs to be tomorrow. With all the brouhaha, my Yellowstone plans are out the window, and I've got zip on the bench. Judd, a bona fide gourmet chef, is in the group this year, so I better come up with something good. And fast. Given the choice, these guys will sit around the cabin all day, making cream puffs and swapping recipes. If I'm not quick on my feet, they'll dress me in an apron and order me around by my new nickname, Garcon. The only way it might be a good trade is if Judd can deliver Bombe Alaska.

Even if we end up stuck in the cabin for a day, all is not lost. Some of the most memorable Boys' Trip moments happen off the playing field. Some are just plain out of bounds.

Judd is not a hiker, but he's an avid fly fisherman, and Montana is prime country for big fish and big fish tales. He's going through difficult times at the moment, so Glenn invited him on this trip to give him a break from the struggle, a chance to recharge. It's another example of Hobbit magnanimity.

Judd's good with a fly rod, but his best performance was orchestrating the cabin kitchen dressed in his gray flannel onesie with the dual relief flaps. The same type Jed Clampett wore. A guy needs to be pretty comfortable with his manhood to wear one of those things. Or just not give a hoot what anybody thinks.

When he wasn't cooking, Judd took to patrolling the cabin brandishing Glenn's antique rifle. And a sneer. You got a problem with tonight's dinner? Well do ya, punk? The guy was a great cook. Unforgettable. There goes the Rube wandering off course again. Back to my trip planning challenge . . .

With Yellowstone off limits, I need a quick change of target. I break out my topo map and scan the Absaroka-Beartooth Range just north of the national park. There are several sizable peaks in the range, but I'm drawn to one called Emigrant.

Emigrant Peak towers over Paradise Valley in southwest Montana. This beautiful area is the setting for several well-known movies, including *The Horse Whisperer* and *A River Runs through It*. At 10,921 feet, Emigrant is not the highest or the most difficult peak in the range, but it carries bragging rights. If there is a poster boy of southwest Montana, a peak that can rival the glory of Yellowstone, Emigrant is it. Not that the Rube and this ragtag bunch are looking for glory.

The Hobbit is an attorney and a judge with a healthy respect for jurisprudence and prudence of the regular variety. He is up for a challenge, but not into crazy risk taking. With his son Sam joining us on the hike, Glenn will be even more cautious than usual. He will be prepared with an arsenal of objections to any hike he deems unsafe or even slightly beyond the pale. I will need to curb my adolescent impulses and be on my best behavior. Act like an adult for a change. After a long day of travel, tonight is not the time to engage the Hobbit in a debate on the virtues of peak-bagging. I will have to make my case in the morning.

As expected, in the morning, the Hobbit's briefcase is overflowing with arguments against Emigrant Peak. His litany of defenses includes: too high, too far, too late, and too much snow. Tippecanoe and Tyler too. Come up with something shorter and easier, Rube. The angel on my right shoulder whispers, "Think about it, Rube. The guy is a lawyer. He argues for a living. He's also a lawyer with a gun. You don't have a prayer against the diminutive but mighty barrister."

I have a few weapons of my own, however. While not nearly as learned or as eloquent, the Rube is rarely outdone in stubbornness. My darker side imp seizes the initiative. My first appeal is to the Hobbit's ego.

In my most earnest manner, I make my case. "Just think about it, Glenn. Hiking on Emigrant, we will be treading on the same ground that Brad Pitt and Robert Redford have trod. Sheez, Mister Mayor, you could place your hairy Hobbit feet in the footsteps of *Jeremiah Johnson*."

I forget that Hobbits have outsized feet and undersized egos. Hobbits are a noble, humble breed, so the ego play doesn't work. Time is of the essence, so I decide to skip over the niceties and go straight for the Vulcan pinkie pinch.

I ask for permission to come in for a little close talk, man-to-Hobbit. "May I approach the bench, your highness?"

Glenn waves me into his personal bubble. "It's your honor. And yes, you may."

I lean in, my voice practically a whisper. "You know, Glenn, your reputation as a tough guy and a legendary frontier lawman would take a serious hit if people were to find out about your collusion with SpongeBob."

His look says it all. "You wouldn't."

I grimace. "It will be tough to command the respect of a hostile defendant or an opposing counselor if they know SquarePants is abiding under that impressive judicial robe of yours. There could be anarchy in the courtroom."

I am referring, not to a nefarious conspiracy, but to the Hobbit's proclivity for SpongeBob jockey shorts. In any event, he relents, and it's *dealus dunnum*. Emigrant it is.

In what is becoming a troublesome trend, the boys and I are getting another perilously late start. The Rube and his band of merry men don't approach the trailhead until noon. The weather has been dicey all morning, and we might yet be rained or snowed out. This dirt road is becoming treacherous, and the Hobbit is getting antsy piloting a two-wheel-drive junker where only four-wheelers belong. I'm thinking we better just get out of the van. We can at least poke around a bit before giving up.

We clamber out of the rig and start walking up the rutted road. After a quarter-mile, we spot the trailhead in a meadow beside Gold Prize Creek. We begin our march up the trail with Hobbit and son in the lead, followed by Chad, Roger, Judd, and me. Roger is our designated sheriff, toting the firearm. I take special note of the bear warning poster at the trailhead. No worries here. The neighborhood bears have nothing to fear from this group.

For the first mile and a quarter, the hike is a pleasant stroll beside the creek and doesn't require a serious level of exertion.

It's a good time to review the Rube's theory of incrementalism as applied to hiking before the going starts to get tough.

Judd, the fisherman-chef, is not fired up for this hiking thing, but he's tagging along for our sake. Glenn also is hobbling a bit with a balky knee. Whenever you have a guy or two not "all in" on a trek, the best response is to acknowledge their concerns. Nod in agreement and say something like, "Mm, hmm. I hear you. But we're not going to do anything you're not capable of." Encourage them, and just keep moving.

In most cases, the hesitant guy just needs a shot of confidence. Each milestone he reaches makes the next one more attainable. From his new vantage point, it won't seem quite so far or quite so high to the next one. The Brotherhood keeps moving onward sometimes pushing and sometimes pulling each other upward. Even with a really smart guy, even when he knows exactly what's happening, it's very hard to reverse the forward momentum. Deep down, he doesn't want to stop it. He wants to go further than he thought he could, higher than he believed he was able.

After another quarter-mile, the trail turns away from the creek, but the slope is still gentle and conditions are mild. The conversation among the boys is good, and the living is easy. Before we know it, we've been trekking an hour and a half, and we've climbed several hundred feet. We reach the saddle separating the foothills from the steeper, more rugged terrain. The clouds have lifted, and we get our first view of a snow-capped Emigrant Peak under dappled sunshine. It's inspiring to have a goal in sight, a vision of where you hope to be or what you hope to achieve. The peak is magnificent if not a tad intimidating. The Hobbit is struggling with his knee and with his sore feet, but he is comparatively giddy when he pledges his next goal is the snow line. The snow line is about halfway to the summit, a worthy goal, indeed. The summit fever is working.

After a mile and a half and another five hundred-foot gain, we reach the broad grassy plateau overlooking Paradise Valley. From up here, the view across the valley unfolds west to the snow-covered peaks of the Gallatin Range. The plateau is the limit for Judd. For a guy who would rather be tying flies or whipping up a soufflé, it has been a stouthearted effort. A guy will endure much for the sake of fellowship.

Roger will hang back with Judd and scout for grizzly. Roger does a decent impression of one of the gunslingers in the film, *The Apple Dumpling Gang*. I hope he's carrying more than one round in his shirt pocket.

The snow line is another four hundred feet up from the plateau. The Hobbit is intent on making good on his pledge, so even though he's in obvious pain, he labors up the grassy knoll behind Sam, Chad, and me.

At the hilltop, it would be appropriate to perform some sort of a transfer ritual where the Hobbit can lay down the law for our attempt at the summit. It would go something like this:

Hobbit: "Raise your right hand and repeat after me. I, Rube, do solemnly swear to do nothing stupid, to always look both ways, to honor my father and mother, and to be home before dark with all the boys intact." I swear.

With that Sam is officially in charge. Having fulfilled his promise, the Hobbit heads back down to the plateau, no doubt with a sinking feeling in the pit of his trim, always taut gut.

The northwest ridge route gains another 1,500 feet with slopes up to sixty degrees, and it's covered with snow. I'm surprised by how deep and how heavy the stuff is, but more concerned with how heavy my legs are. We are the first hikers to venture up here after the latest storm, so Sam is cutting the trail, postholing in two to three feet of wet snow. He's wearing blue jeans and low-cut sneakers. He digs up a fallen tree branch and uses it as a hiking stick. The staff is a foot taller than he is so he looks like a young Moses wading through a knee-deep sea of manna. He is unstoppable.

The only thing slowing Sam down is waiting for the Rube plodding deliberately about a hundred feet below him and Chad. I'm stopping often, my excuse being I need to take pictures, or unload some other piece of gear no longer worth its weight. Truth is, I can't keep up with them. I'm gassed like I haven't been hiking in a long time. Postholing in deep snow is not a common training exercise for Arizona hiking. But maybe it should be.

After dumping my backpack, there's nothing left to unload. I should dump myself with it. The boys should leave me behind. I have become a burden. I am keeping them from a shot at the summit. Hey, wait a minute. Sam is carrying the wood and a knife. Chad has the fire. They can cobble up enough rocks to build an altar. I had better keep my horns clear of any thickets.

It seems as though a door is being opened for us. The hike had started under the threat of bad weather with the mountain shrouded in clouds. Right now, conditions are glorious, and the sky is as intensely blue as any I've seen in person or on *Planet Earth*.

The fly in the ointment is that it's 4:30 p.m., and we have less than two hours of daylight left. We're above the tree line and the wind has blown most of the snow off the highest reaches of Emigrant. It looks like we're only about five hundred feet below the peak, but there are a few false summits on this route. For me the final pitch will not go quickly. It's a steep scramble on about a forty-degree slope where the loose talus shifts slides under every step. It's time for a different type of summit, so I call Chad over for a meeting of the minds.

At best, we figure it will take me an hour and a half to summit and get back down to this spot. If everything goes perfectly, we'll be hiking the final two hours in the dark.

The boys and I have finished a few long hikes in the dark before, but I've never been entrusted with the safety of a buddy's first born. And in the heart of grizzly territory, no less.

That changes everything. It's one thing to risk an old guy or two, but a young guy with his whole life ahead of him?

Sam not only embodies his father's aspirations, he represents the next generation. Our kids are our best hope for baby boomer redemption. To cause one of these little ones to be lost would be a sin of biblical proportions. To the clear-headed, reasonable guy, the wise choice is self-evident. Rube, the macho mountain cowboy, however, is putting up a ruckus. I'm grasping for any excuse to keep climbing. Didn't I read where Montana is going to daylight saving time this afternoon? That gives us an extra hour.

It's a good thing that Sam is not around to hear me whimpering like a new puppy on his first night away from mama. "Why does it have to be so beautiful?" I grumble-think. It would be way easier to turn back if it were cold and miserable.

Finally, the light breaks through. Rube, making the summit won't change your life. Violating a friend's trust will change your life, and possibly someone else's. And not for the better.

Then Sam proceeds to show me what a True Man, millennial edition, looks like.

He is already a hundred feet up the mountain when Chad and I call him back. He retraces his route, takes his orders, and nods in agreement. Sam then dutifully leads us down the mountain. We make such good time that we meet up with the boys on the plateau, and make the entire return trek before darkness settles in. Emigrant Peak, glowing persimmon in the sunset, provides a memorable backdrop for the drive home.

For the lead dog, cutting a steep trail in new snow is an especially tough trek. Thanks to Sam, the guys who follow have an easier time of it. From Sam, there was not a word of complaint, despite the wet, the cold, the chafing, and the weight of soaked shoes, socks, and soggy, heavy denim. After enduring all that, he had the summit swiped from under him.

Chad and Sam never considered leaving me behind to bag the peak without me. If I were a better man I would have told them to go on ahead and pick me up on their way down. I'm grateful for the display of solidarity. I hope I mentioned it.

Sam' biggest accomplishment, though, was delivering us back to father Hobbit on time, thereby making the Rube look good and responsible. No easy task. True to his humble roots, he isn't looking for praise and won't take any credit for it.

Sam schooled me in humility, obedience, and leadership. Not with words, but by example. If we elders spent less energy pontificating about the next generation, we might just learn something from them. Besides, we baby boomers are the original lost generation. Who are we to preach? If we think our kids are lost, it's because we showed them the way

INTERLUDE: MOVIN' ON UP

The word *emigrant* means one who moves away from his native country to make his home in another place. The human soul, though born into the natural world, is created for the spiritual realm. We are ultimately destined for a different kingdom. All souls are bound to be emigrants.

The quest to go further and higher on the mountain is like the invitation of Christ and his Church to go deeper in faith. The scriptures and the catechism contain the maps and charts for the journey. Books and maps are great as far as they go, but they can't convey the scope and magnitude of something as glorious as the great mountain or the depth and richness of faith. For it to penetrate to the core of his being, a man must experience real things in person.

Beginning to study the Bible is like the first glimpse of a great mountain on the horizon, intimidating. It's so high, so big, and so distant. A guy thinks he could never scale it and never comprehend it. Many guys don't even make an attempt. Other men are so focused on what is immediately before them that they don't even see the mountain. They're too short-sighted to even look to the horizon.

Instead of striving for the upper reaches of understanding and virtue, we set about building our own mountains by piling up possessions, attachments, payments, obligations, and worries. Our world is so busy that there's no time left for spiritual pursuits. The older we get, the greater the inertia and the resistance to a lived faith.

This is where a fellowship like the Boys' Trip fills the breach by putting the wisdom of the ancient Church into action. A brotherhood of like-minded pals can challenge a guy to chisel away some of that boulder he's carrying on his back. He can go higher and faster when he's lighter on his feet. A guy needs to revisit his maps and charts often and to recalculate when he gets off trail.

A glorious day on a mountain like Emigrant Peak encompasses all the stuff of adventure: challenge, exertion, encouragement, achievement, and reward. It might be the closest thing to a slice of heaven on earth.

GERONIMO JACK

Whoa, what was that? My mind is drifting when I'm nearly blown into the weeds. It's dead calm this morning, so it can't be a desert dust devil that takes me by surprise. It's the turbo exhaust from another runner. A runner much faster than me.

Reach 11 is a recreation area where I run almost every week. It's practically my own private slice of desert solitude. I'm usually alone out here, so encountering any other human can be startling, especially one with wings for feet. Though he was practically a blur, I have an odd feeling that I've seen him before. Who was that guy?

I serve at church as a greeter, welcoming people to Mass each week. It used to be that I would do almost anything to avoid the greeter guy. You know the type. He's the too-friendly guy always inviting men to join something, volunteer for something, or do stuff the typical guy doesn't want to do. Nobody should be allowed to be that cheerful. Now I am the greeter guy, yet another strange twist in an unlikely journey.

It's a couple of weeks after the trail running encounter, and I'm in the foyer dealing bulletins and wisecracks before

Mass when the light bulb in my belfry flickers. It used to be a bell. Holy cow, it's him.

I've seen this guy with his family most Sundays for at least ten years, but we've never shared more than two words: hello and welcome. But that's no different from any of a hundred guys I see here weekly and never make an effort to befriend. Most guys seem too busy for anything more than the casual greeting. They appear to have important things to do, and their time is always short. And I'm a chicken.

The Rube, however, is different. He doesn't seem to be bound by the same rules of manly decorum. He can be fearless since he doesn't have an image to protect. Most guys are not his friends now, so he doesn't worry about losing them. The Rube has no problem stumbling into a stranger's personal space.

Before Flash can slip past me, I blurt, "Hey, it's you! You're the guy I saw running in Reach 11 a couple weeks ago. You nearly blew my doors off."

Flash takes my intrusion in stride. "Yeah, I run in the Reach, so that's entirely possible. It's funny, though, I don't remember you."

"I move pretty slowly. You might have mistaken me for a rock. You were going almost supersonic. I'm guessing you're a runner, but are you a hiker too?"

"Yeah, I hike a little." Then he speeds off after his family.

Men are befuddling creatures. Sometimes surprising, but often predictable.

A churchgoing guy can easily slip in and out for years without being detected. If he walks fast enough and appears purposeful, he won't be asked to volunteer or commit to anything. He also seems to have telekinetic powers. If he's cornered, he can make his cell phone ring anytime he needs a quick escape. It seems like the typical average guy wants only the minimum required dose of religion, if he wants any religion at all. Then he can get out and get on with his real life.

Flash doesn't seem like one of those guys. Still, it takes work to get a few words out of him every week. He's a quiet, private, family man, more likely to run for the hills than to run for mayor. His name is Jack, and he indeed hikes a little. Actually, he's a certified, card-carrying peak bagger.

If not for that one fleeting encounter in an unlikely place, I might never know this most fascinating character. Author, C. S. Lewis, proposed in *The Weight of Glory* that there is no such thing as an ordinary man, only fellow immortals. Looking ahead, Jack might be who Lewis had in mind. This guy would hold his own against just about any action superhero in the comic and movie universe.

I'm no peak bagger, but when a named peak is tantalizingly close, it's hard for a hiker to resist the lure of the summit. McDowell Peak has been whispering my name for a while now. There's no established trail to the peak, and, though the summit is off limits to hikers, that restriction could never contain a guy like Jack. Who better to school a rookie like me on the art of off-trail desert peak bagging?

When I mention McDowell Peak to Jack, of course, he's done it. He says he'll take me up there some weekend if he can squeeze it into his schedule. But that's a big 'if'. Jack's in hot pursuit of personal records this year for both elevation gain and new summits. He's in a competition with another elite hiker. It's what peak baggers do, I guess. I'm sure he'll forget all about me.

About a month later, at 5:00 a.m. one cold winter Sunday, I receive a text from Jack to meet him at the Bell Pass trailhead in an hour. Jack, apparently, is different. When he says he will do something, he doesn't forget it; he commits to it.

When I arrive at the trailhead, Jack greets me like a ghost from the darkness of the vacant dirt parking lot, his bright yellow shirt glowing in my headlights. He's apologetic.

"Sorry about the late notice. I didn't know exactly when we'd get back."

I can't believe he's actually here.

"No worries, Jack. I'm always up early. Where are you back from?"

Jack pauses from filling his hydration pack. "Me and a couple of guys had a little adventure in the canyon Friday and Saturday."

Jack is fresh from a thirty-mile expedition in the Grand Canyon with an elevation gain in the ten thousand-foot range. He arrived back in the Valley after midnight, and here he is ready to go again five hours later. This is what squeezing a schedule looks like.

Bell Pass is the closest trail to McDowell Peak, and it's a tough trail for the average hiker. It's barely a warm-up for Jack. He babies me for the first two miles, just to be sociable, and then he shifts his motor out of idle. At three miles, I'm laboring up to the saddle, the high point of the trail. Jack's been out of sight for at least twenty minutes. From here to the McDowell summit it's another eight hundred feet of gain and a mile of scrambling in the nasty, scratchy, prickly, venomous stuff that gives desert hiking a bad name. In other words, it's gorgeous up there.

Squinting toward the summit, I spot Jack three-quarters of the way up the mountain, gobbling up obstacles like Pac-man. And I thought he was going to hold my hand. Maybe I should just wait here for him. There's a stone bench over there that looks good right now.

Jack is supposed to be teaching me something about serious hiking, and at this point the best grade I can hope for is an Incomplete. My better angel spurs me on. After forty minutes of careful scrambling in pursuit of Jack, I'm just below the summit ridge. There's no sign of him.

I pause for a moment. It's quiet enough up here I could swear I hear a voice coming from the shadow of a boulder outcropping, or is it from the shadows of my mind? The words are familiar.

"To be, or not to be, that is the question: Whether 'tis nobler in the mind to suffer the slings and arrows of outrageous fortune, or to take arms against a sea of troubles . . ."

Who else but Jack? As a lad, Jack's father had him memorize the entire *Hamlet* soliloquy. The classic work still resides in his consciousness like a prayer in the mind of a religious aspirant. Many prayers roll off the tongue like poetic verse, and one couldn't do much better than Shakespeare. Jack also writes poetry in his spare time. Along with everything else he is, Jack is a Renaissance man.

When he spots me, he calls out, "I was beginning to wonder if I would be performing a rescue today."

"You may yet get your chance," I retort.

Instead of being impatient or annoyed, Jack is calm and relaxed. I've heard that reading poetry can have a calming influence. That must work only for smart guys because most poems are puzzling and mysterious to me, which only makes me more restless. In addition to hiking at a higher level, Jack thinks and reflects on a deeper level.

After Jack escorts me the rest of the way to the summit, he snaps a few photos.

"I document all my hikes online," he explains.

"Cool," I reply. "Thanks for including me in a picture. Nobody will believe I hiked with Geronimo Jack without photographic evidence. So, this is all just for the record?"

He nods. "I'm on target for five hundred peaks this year."

I'm rightly sarcastic. "Well, you couldn't have done this one without me. Glad I could help you out."

Though peak bagging is serious business, Jack cracks a smile and winks, "You're welcome."

Looking down on a panorama I've never seen, I'm feeling pretty good about myself. "Thanks for waiting on me, Jack. Awesome view. Is this about as good as it gets?"

When he raises his right arm, bent at the elbow, I'm hoping for a pat on the back. Instead his posture recalls a maestro cueing up the string section of the orchestra.

Wait a minute. Jack is a black belt martial arts instructor. He could take me down with an arm lock and a leg sweep. It'll be a long fall from here. Instead, with a pretty fair impression of Mister Miyagi from the film *The Karate Kid*, Jack traces a slow 270-degree arc in the air, marking three points, as if on a compass.

"Besides McDowell, there's Drinkwater, East End, and Thompson Peak."

I'm enthralled, "This area is huge, Sensei. There are many miles between those peaks. Have you done any of the others?"

I've gotten better at recognizing a dumb question pretty quickly when I hear it, not fast enough when I speak it.

Jack nods. "Yeah. I've done all four." He pauses. "On the same day, one hike." He smiles and adds, "That was a pretty good day."

I'm chastened. So much for my vain desire for empty praise. To Jack, a good day is when a guy is all in, when he's given his very best effort to whatever task is at hand. He must have learned from tough teachers and trainers who don't believe in doling out easy rewards. The ultra-hiker must learn to draw his fuel from a deeper well. Jack might have learned from Chief Geronimo himself.

Hiking is like life. For a guy to get ahead in his field he must continually meet the challenge of his competitor. At times the competitor is the clock. Other times, the trail, and sometimes, himself. How does a radical hiker like Jack find a worthy hike hard enough to test him?

The following week, I arrest Jack in the church entry for his answer.

"Where do you go for a challenge around here, Jack? You have a career and a family, so you can't be running off to Death Valley every weekend."

Jack keeps walking. "I like to hike deep into the Mazzies." Then he says over his shoulder, "Oh, and when I go to Death Valley, I take the car." Renaissance men can be funny.

The Matatzal Wilderness is to Geronimo Jack what the desert proving grounds are to General Motors. Though less than two hours from the valley, it's an area so wild and rugged that it sees very little human activity. The few trails it has are rough, and most hikers are not grizzly man enough to endure their punishment. Those who do are allowed to call the mountains by their nickname, the Mazzies.

A few years ago, one of Jack's hiking buddies, GPS Joe, vanished in the Mazzies in the vicinity of Sheep Mountain. Joe is presumed dead, but no trace of him has been found. Ever since Joe went missing, Jack periodically leads a search party to the area, hoping to locate some evidence of Joe, anything that would give his family a sense of peace. Like Jack, GPS Joe enjoyed hiking solo. He was alone when he disappeared.

In Joe's memory, Jack has a standing offer to personally guide anyone desiring to hike Sheep Mountain. This is no small matter. Sheep Mountain is a tough, full day's commitment even for the fittest hiker. Is this what a true friendship looks like? To remain faithful to a pal when it's inconvenient and difficult, when others have long since bailed out? Jack even offered to guide me up on Sheep Mountain. I thought about it only briefly, I'm not proud to admit, before declining. I don't think I'm man enough.

So where does a man find the kind of steadfast strength to remain a faithful friend when a guy becomes a burden or even after he's long dead and gone? Where does Jack's perseverance come from? His commitment?

Many guys spend their entire lives making shallow acquaintances and very few lasting friendships. I'm among the worst. A guy doesn't have to be lost or dead to drop from the Rube's radar.

For ten years, I met weekly for coffee with a great pal, Leland the Zealot. Leland had a life-changing influence on me, so when he moved to Indiana, I vowed to stay in touch. I actually meant it at the time. It's now been over three years since I've had any contact with LTZ. Nice effort, Rube. From what I know of other guys, they're not much better. But that doesn't give me a Get Out of Jail Free pass. Men always compare ourselves to each other, but we didn't get that habit from God. I haven't come across any evidence that he judges us against each other. He doesn't grade on a curve.

Men who have it too comfortable have a hard time committing to anything, including genuine friendship. This is an age-old problem with every generation. The True Man is a friend who fulfills his promises in and out of season when the harvest is abundant and when it's scarce. He satisfies his commitments to the best of his ability, not the minimum required to get by.

We're supposed to model ourselves after Jesus. But could a guy ever live up to God's impossibly high standard for friendship? The Lord promised, "I am with you always to the close of the age" (Mt 28:20). A guy could look to Geronimo Jack, and he'd be on the right track.

INTERLUDE: TAG! YOU'RE IT

Ask a guy when he felt most like a man, and you get answers that have little to do with things like being a good husband, a good father, or a man of God. We associate manliness with stuff like winning a Super Bowl ring, bagging a trophy elk in Alaska, or saving the neighbor's dog from a burning house.

These are the stories a guy relives time and again. Indelible manly memories often involve an event where a guy survived some dire danger or where he overcame a challenge out in the wild. The elements of risk and adventure seem to be important parts of our nature as men. Deep down we know we're supposed to stand strong against forces that would do us harm or endanger our loved ones. We're built for heroism. We seem to understand it in the natural realm. Too many guys don't see it that way when it comes to the spiritual world. The unseen world is unreal.

The typical guy doesn't view life as a quest for truth and holiness or as a heroic struggle against evil. The idea of helping his family reach eternal glory in the next life sounds like a fairy tale, science fiction, or something from the comic book universe. That hero stuff is source material for children's books, Hollywood, TV, and video games. It's not the real world.

My pal Jack has many characteristics of an action hero. Not bogus superhuman powers, but genuine supernatural skills. The type of character traits a guy could emulate in his real-world life. Jack is a man of his word, a man of integrity. He is a loyal friend even when a situation seems hopeless. He believes in driving himself to deliver his very best effort. He has perseverance, devotion, and trustworthiness.

For the typical average guy, his real world consists of work and family life where he's pulled in too many directions at once, and his time is always short. He handles his leisure time the same way, packing it full of activities and busyness and leaving little room for meaningful relationships. Becoming a real friend seems like too much work. Because there is no immediate payback in religion, he leaves zero time for things unseen. For relaxation, it's so easy to escape into a plethora of fantasy worlds. Don't ask him to carve out time for prayer, scripture study, or a men's group. Too busy.

And I am no better than the typical average guy. Tag! I'm it.

But for a stroke of Providence and the Rube's willingness to risk appearing foolish, I wouldn't know this most inspiring character, this real-life action hero, Jack.

How many other fellow immortals are waiting for you to make the first move? For you to be bold and forward?

How many men are languishing spiritually, waiting for an invitation from you?

How much richer will we all be to engage as brothers in the great adventure of faith?

A shared experience is a treasure that makes for a lifelong friendship. You don't need to sail around the world in a dinghy. There are plenty of risks right close to home. Even a modest Boys' Trip can produce the stories and memories of a lifetime. Get a couple pals together and get out.

FLIRTING WITH DANGER

I t seems to me that the slot canyon is a paradox of the highest order. First, God creates great beauty in the mountains and plateaus. And then, by their systematic destruction, he fashions another type of intricate and fascinating beauty. Creation by destruction. The slot canyon is the fruit of the relentless wearing away of a vast landmass by rainwater runoff, the gradual erosion of a colossal stone. Water is not a resident in the slot. It's a visitor, by turns a gracious house guest bearing gifts and a malevolent one bringing destruction.

Slot canyon hiking is a different breed of animal where a single variable trumps all the various factors that go into planning a trip. When there is a chance of rain anywhere in the watershed, the prudent hiker stays out of the slots. His plans and preparations must go back in the pack for another day. A good trip planner better have his deck of Man Cards ready for a rainy day.

Buckskin Gulch in southern Utah is perhaps the longest and deepest slot canyon on the planet. The watershed for Buckskin stretches fifty miles north to Bryce National Park, draining streams all across the Paria Plateau. Moments into a thunderstorm, Buckskin becomes a storm tunnel. It's a bit

like the Golden Gate Bridge. Vehicles come to it from many
roads, stacking up on each other. To cross the bay on wheels
there's only one way. To the slot canyon adventurer, rain is
his mortal enemy; a current weather forecast his crucial ally.

It's day one of a highly anticipated Boys' Trip, and we're
going after a prized slot canyon trophy. After a half-day drive
from Phoenix, Pierce, Chad, and I arrive at the Paria Ranger
Station in southern Utah, command central for slot canyon
country.

Rain is a big deal to people in these parts, especially for
park rangers. They monitor the weather every day, but not
on a flat screen TV with scrolling, up-to-the-minute updates,
high-tech satellite images, and maps. The weather forecast is
scribbled on a notebook page pinned to the front door. They
must have seen the Rube coming. Rangers can't physically close
down the trails, but they want to be sure a weather warning
reaches a bumbling Griswold even if the on-duty ranger is in
the bathroom. Scribbled on the note are the words: *No rain
today, 30% tomorrow (Friday), higher on Saturday.*

The Boys' Trip is always on a tight schedule, so this weather
update is inconvenient at best. My original plan for tomorrow
was a long loop hike, first through Buckskin for twelve miles
and then seven miles up the Paria River Canyon. The Paria
is not a slot canyon, so we'd have the faster, easier hike at the
end of the day. But Buckskin is now off limits for tomorrow.
If I'm to abide by the strict rules for prudent conduct, we
have today or what remains of it to bag Buckskin. And strictly
speaking, that's why we're here.

To determine the actual conditions in the slot, hikers
must rely on word of mouth reports from other hikers. The
weather's been unsettled over the past few days, and nobody's
hiked in Buckskin all week. At least no one has filed a report.
We'll just have to find out for ourselves while always obeying
the rules of prudence, of course.

There is another entry to Buckskin that could save us some time; Wire Pass, a tributary that carves out a shallow canyon that funnels into Buckskin from the south. We can do Wire Pass today, and after two miles, intersect with Buckskin. We can go as deep into the gulch as time allows and get back out before dark. It will require some resourcefulness to get to Buckskin today, but it wouldn't be on anyone's life list if it were too easy.

It's 2:00 p.m. when we head out from the Wire Pass trailhead. The first half mile is a hot, dry walk in mostly packed sand similar to any other desert wash. A first-time slot canyon hiker can't really be ready for what awaits him as the slot deepens. One minute, he's in the glorious, vivid sunshine of the high desert. The next, he's in what feels like the foreign world of a secret mountain hideaway, sort of a bat cave in the boulders.

My first slot canyon experience was at Antelope Canyon, a popular tourist destination on the Navajo Nation in Arizona. Eleven hikers were killed by a flash flood in Lower Antelope in 1997. Now, nobody gets near Antelope without reservations and a Navajo-approved tour guide. Don't misunderstand, Antelope Canyon is awe-inspiring, but it's hardly wild anymore. It's another tourist experience. This is different. Buckskin Gulch is a world away from tour busses, fashion models, and photo shoots. The Rube and his pals have the gulch all to ourselves. This is wild.

From the shadows inside the slot, a rush of cold air hits us like stepping into a walk-in refrigerator. In Wire Pass, there's no sign of the recent rains. The canyon is dry, having funneled its runoff into the deeper gash. Wire Pass connects to the gulch near its tightest segment. At its confluence with Buckskin, the atmosphere takes a turn to the dark side. In spots the slot is barely ten feet wide, and the canyon walls grow to hundreds of feet high. The sandstone seems noticeably darker, or maybe it's just my frame of mind. The gulch is warning us that we're approaching forbidden territory.

The sky above is barely a sliver of gray. In here, the dicey weather has left its evidence. Buckskin is peppered with shallow puddles and deeper pools of cold, still water. For a half mile, we maneuver up on the banks around them, but after that, we must muck through them. The mud sucks my river sandals off my heels with every other step. During the next half mile of this slow trudging, my thoughts are not on the awesome peace and solitude of this place, but on the dangers of flash floods and quicksand. It's not fair.

Slot canyon hikes are dangerous due to the risk of flash flooding and the limited opportunities for escape. But the slot canyon is seductive. With clear skies overhead, a hiker is tempted to think he's in the clear. Miles away, a cloudburst can send a stealth torrent surging his way. There is no communication in the slot, so the approaching rumble will be his only notice. Weather warnings, GPS, radio, and cell signals don't work in here. Once he enters a slot, a hiker, prudent or not, is on his own. But are you taking this prudence thing a little too far, Rube? Sure, hikers die in slot canyons. But people die everywhere. Chad got hit by a bus once on his way to work. Still it makes me wonder, do guardian angels have a limit on the number of saves?

Both my mood and the atmosphere are growing ever darker. Flash floods in this gulch carry dangerous debris in a wall of water twenty feet tall or higher. I imagine a ball of debris the size of the rolling boulder in the Indiana Jones thrill ride at Disneyland. Except in here there's no magic wand or fairy dust to make it all go away.

I've only seen quicksand in old Western TV shows where the outlaw is slowly swallowed by the soup until only his black hat remains. Get real, Rube. That's Hollywood. To escape from quicksand, a guy needs another guy on firm ground with a sturdy stick. Quicksand kills when the victim panics and struggles frantically until exhausted. This muck is not deep enough to be quicksand, but it could be an evil cousin. It won't kill us on its own. It'll slow us down enough for a flash flood to claim us. Flypaper doesn't kill flies. They die of starvation, or they pull their own wings off in the struggle.

Desperate hikers stuck in slot canyons have been known to gnaw their own arms off with a dull pocketknife. Hollywood made a movie about that too, but it was a true story. And it happened not far from here. This isn't a carefree afternoon stroll in the garden of Eden. Oh, yeah. It's a Boys' Trip.

It would be good to have a long, stout stick, just in case. The only thing in here besides puddles, mud, and boulders is a tree trunk jammed in the slot over our heads, evidence that the flash flood danger is not all in my mind.

I cast a glance back at Chad. "How high up do you reckon that tree trunk is?" My voice swirling around the slot sounds like reverb on the stereo.

Chad cranes his neck and squints. "Forty, maybe fifty feet, I guess."

"Forty feet is a lot of water." I gulp.

In a flash flood, an unfortunate soul in this spot would have mere seconds to scramble to high ground on sheer, steep, sandstone walls, walls worn so smooth that nothing grows on them or sticks to them. Spiderman himself would have a fifty-fifty shot at making it. The Rube is a sure bet for becoming a pinball. My inner peace is leaking out.

From Wire Pass, Buckskin is twelve miles long, and there's only one escape hatch at the eight-mile point, Middle Exit. God help you if you happen to be miles from Middle Exit when the heavens open up. I've never heard a wall of water before, but is that a distant rumble I hear? Maybe it's thunder. That's not as bad as a wall of water, but it's still not good. I scan the sheer canyon walls for a ledge or a way to scramble up to higher ground.

Pierce is looking around, too. "How far are we from Middle Exit?" Inquiring minds want to know.

"I figure it's at least three miles that way," I point deeper into the gulch. It's after 3:00 p.m. At this rate, we won't get there before dark.

I feel a drop of moisture on my arm. Then another. It's sprinkling. Get a grip, Rube. This is no time to panic. "The forecast said no rain today," I snort. "Aren't weathermen in Utah any better than forecasters anyplace else?" I'm hoping Chad, the elder and wiser, will ease my mind.

"They do make mistakes," Chad says, raking the slop from his boot with his hiking pole. "They're not the pope." He's not helping. Chad is an open-minded Presbyterian, and his comment is light hearted not confrontational.

I'm ready to get out of here, while the getting is good. Fortunately for me, Pierce and Chad don't take much convincing. We turn about and start working our way back toward Wire Pass. It's best to take our chips off the table and live to play the slots another day. There's more than one way to skin a buck.

The rain holds off overnight, and the next day I'm still flirting with Buckskin Gulch. I'm not ready to surrender. We can reverse directions and hike seven miles down the wider Paria River canyon and get into Buckskin at its east end. Lucky for me, the boys are in a forgiving mood. The hike down the Paria is wide open, so we make good time to the confluence with Buckskin. Though it's a new day, the gulch seems in the same foul, dark mood.

Two miles in from the confluence, we encounter the largest obstacle in the entire Gulch, a boulder jam over three stories tall. This is where Buckskin is its deepest and darkest, where a wall of floodwater meets its first significant resistance. A flash flood rolls unimpeded for over ten miles through what amounts to a high-speed flume before crashing here in a violent collision of water, tree trunks, rocks, and debris. This ain't Splash Mountain.

There's a rope in place to assist with the climb over the rocks, but the boulder pile is not the steepest obstacle. The psychological barrier is far more formidable. And, oh yeah, there's still that pesky chance of rain. It's radically foolish to be in this spot today. Since I'm responsible for two other guys, I can add the offense of imprudence to my rap sheet. Prudence is not a secular concept. It's one of the Church's four cardinal virtues, so it's pivotal to the development of other virtues. This is serious business.

I'm not sure whether it's prudence or cowardice, but the Rube sees the light. We turn around and head back, this time for good. We leave the deepest and darkest stretch of Buckskin for braver or more foolish men than us.

That evening we're sitting in the Paria Outpost enjoying the Friday night Texas BBQ. The Outpost is a local favorite, and folks drive from miles around for the weekend specials. To ward off the cold each fall, the Outpost's proprietors enclose the large patio with heavy sheets of clear plastic almost as thick as Plexiglas.

Chad, Pierce, and I are relaxing on the patio with all manner of farmers, ranchers, and cowboys when the storm hits. The wind is so fierce, it blows out all the patio windows, and rain is coming in sideways. We grab our drinks and plates, and scurry inside. The rickety, rustic outpost shudders like it's going to lift off.

We settle into a tight, corner table inside the dining room. I shiver. "You know, boys, if we'd stuck with my original plan, we would've gone into Buckskin early this morning from Wire Pass." I pause. "We'd still be in the belly of the beast right now."

Chad is a doctor, and he can be analytical. "What is it, twelve miles long? In those mucky conditions, we might make a mile an hour if we're lucky."

Pierce nods. "That's twelve hours. This group doesn't start anything until at least 10 a.m." Pierce knows our history. He's lived it. "It's 7 p.m. now. We'd have three hours yet to go."

I gulp. "We'd be getting to the boulder jam right about now."

Just in time to greet the flash flood waters.

The outpost door strains against its frame, and paper plates are sailing like Frisbees. The wind propels a pair of rain rivulets drag racing across the window. The realization comes to the three of us at once. We shake our heads in unison. "We're history."

Our modified adventure doesn't come with bragging rights. We can't say we conquered Buckskin Gulch. We got just the head and the tail, but the better ends of what could have been a bad bargain. I don't know how things would have turned out had we made a different choice, but from where I sit, I wouldn't trade places with anyone still in Buckskin tonight. They're going to need more than just our prayers. But that's a good place to start.

If there's any consolation for me, the two words, radical and foolish, are tags also attached to Christ and his original followers. Does my faith ever feel dangerous? If not, does that mean I'm not following Christ closely enough? I'm afraid none of us are yet models of truly faithful men, ready for the life of radical discipleship come hell or high water. Either we think we have too much to live for, or we think there is nothing worth dying for.

I'm not going into places where I'm really uncomfortable, where it takes crazy courage and radical love to take the next step. I've been leaving those places for men far holier than me. The kind of men who first sell everything they own. But ultimately it is the most prudent path for the life of the soul. To my stubborn mind, it doesn't seem fair that the radical, foolish path is ultimately the most prudent. Another paradox of the highest order.

INTERLUDE: THE MUCK STOPS HERE

The prospect of a thrill entices men out to the edge of danger, but when our physical nature is threatened, we're quick to retreat. Retreat doesn't feel daring or heroic. It feels safe. When we exceed the bounds of prudence in the wild, nature can be merciless and unforgiving. A guy can die out there.

What about the thrill of sin when we're lured into activities dangerous to our souls? Places we know we shouldn't go? Are we blind to the storm clouds overhead? Do we ignore the warning signs? Because of our disordered nature, spiritual risk doesn't carry the same sense of urgency. We figure we'll have time to get holy later. For now, we just want to have fun. We presume we'll have a chance to repent and turn back to God. Isn't it foolhardy to extend more respect to the forces of nature than we give to their author?

An ill-prepared or foolish hiker might pay a severe price for exceeding the limits of prudence. Likewise, when we separate ourselves from God through sin, there is a price to pay. Our souls are in constant peril without a connection to God's grace, which is like an intravenous drip. The Lord doesn't guarantee safety from physical harm, but he does promise deliverance from spiritual destruction. Despite the promise, I'm reluctant to go deeper into a relationship and obedience to Christ, afraid of what he might require of me. How will I have to change? What must I give up? What am I willing to lose?

The man seeking ultimate truth asks himself a different question. And it's not, "Do I feel lucky?" The question is, "What do I stand to gain if I pray, 'Not my will, Lord, but yours'?"

The Lord says he came that we might have lives of abundance (cf. Jn 10:10).

Why don't I trust him?

RINSE AND REPEAT

P erfect trips are boring. Don't misunderstand; the goal of even a hack, amateur adventure guide is to set up a cool trip where everyone will have a good experience. However, there are certain things a guy could never plan for, so a good guide learns to be flexible and go with the flow. If a trip never went wrong, we wouldn't have *Planes, Trains and Automobiles,* and that would be a tragedy.

A couple years after our Lees Ferry adventure I think enough water has passed under the bridge that we should try another kayak trip. Give the Colorado River another chance. The east end of the Grand Canyon wasn't too kind to us, but that's no reason to hold a grudge. The western end of the canyon, just below Hoover Dam, is called the Black Canyon of the Colorado River. Several commercial rafting companies ply their trade here, putting in below the dam and floating downriver, smooth and easy. They spice things up with a few short hikes to nearby waterfalls and hot springs. They make sure everyone is nice and comfortable. Where's the fun in that? As you know, the Rube earns his bacon by going against the flow. If there is a way to make a thing harder, the Rube will find it.

I reserve three kayaks at Willow Beach marina twelve miles below the dam. Our destination is a beach and hot springs nine miles upstream. Maynard, Pierce, and I will paddle upstream, relax in the hot springs, and camp a night on the beach. A trip like this is as good or as bad as the mood of the weather. An upstream paddle is just a good workout as long as the wind cooperates. If it turns cranky, that's another story. This time the weather is ideal, the water is smooth, and the upstream paddle is a breeze.

We reach the beach before nightfall, and we have the hot springs to ourselves. We float downriver the next day with time for swimming, fishing, and lounging. Memorable sights along the way include a clear blue lagoon with a cave and a family of bighorn sheep making their way down the red cliffs to the river. See how boring this is?

Lest you think it's pure fiction, not everything is perfect. I don't sleep in a tent, so I spread out my pad on the beach under the stars. Around midnight, a rogue cloud dropped thirty seconds of rain on my head. The storm passed so quick I didn't have time to crawl into the tent with Pierce and Maynard. Good thing. After the shower, I'm wide awake. I waste the rest of the night staring at the dim halo on the horizon cast by the lights of Las Vegas. Maynard brought his Book of Psalms with him, and I could have prayed all 150 by headlamp. I might have stored up some treasure in heaven while the revelers on the Strip were placing their bets on Lady Luck. I prayed zero Psalms, choosing as usual to cast my lot with the gamblers.

One of the Rube's cardinal rules of the Boys' Trip is the No Return Principle. The NRP states, thou shalt not repeat a Boys' Trip with a girl. Let me be clear, it's permissible to return to the same location with a girl. Just don't try to replicate the same manly activities. That's not how this works. In case you haven't noticed, girls are different.

I've warned the guys for years about the NRP, and so far, no one has tested it until one day I get a call from Pierce. He has such fond memories of that second Colorado River trip that he wants to go back to the Black Canyon.

On the phone, Pierce sounds excited. "What's the name of that place we went for the kayaks?"

It's always nice to hear that the guys have a good time on these junkets. It's cool that Pierce wants to return on his own and take his son or his brother, Kurt. I'm pleased. "Willow Beach, pal. Let me get the number for you."

I return to the line with the marina's number. "So who are you taking with you?"

Pierce's reply renders me mute. "Mae." Mae is his wife.

I swallow hard and try to regain my composure. I manage a weak reply, "Uh, cool. Have a good time. I hope things go well."

I have an inkling of a disturbance in the force, but bite my tongue. Now is not the time for a lecture. It's not as if an inexorable law of nature has been transgressed. Right? Catholics have big "T" traditions and small "t" traditions. In the book of Rube, the NRP is a small "t" tradition, not a matter of dogma that the faithful are obligated to believe. Maybe it's not such a bad idea to test traditions once in a while.

I don't think anything more about it until our families get together months later to celebrate their new grandbaby. I'm sitting at the other end of the kitchen table with Pierce when I overhear Mae telling Vickie about this disaster she endured with Pierce. I catch just enough of the conversation to know it's about freezing water, mud, pitch dark, and blood.

Pierce is unusually quiet, looking down at his shoes. I make no effort to disguise my eavesdropping as Mae regales Vickie with the gory details. I'm taking it in, nodding and trying to appear sympathetic; after all, it wasn't Mae's fault. She's the victim here.

When I catch Pierce's eye, his face is flushed, and he is clearly chastened. He wasn't going to tell me about his trip, hoping I'd forgotten about it. Pierce should know by now that the Rube's memory is far from perfect, but he files everything away somewhere. A potentially dangerous relic could turn up at any moment.

I let him off the hook for the time being. There will be a better time for this tale. The next gathering of the boys will be the ideal teaching moment.

Pierce's repeat adventure is doomed from the start. When he and Mae arrive at the marina at Willow Beach around noon, he's informed that they can't rent a kayak until 3:00 p.m. due to a change in the marina's rental policy. There's not much to do at Willow Beach for three hours, but Pierce is an optimist. He thinks, no problem. We boys paddled the river in less than three hours the last time. Sunset is not until around 6:30 p.m. We'll be just fine.

There are a few differences this time around. Instead of a single kayak, he's paddling a double kayak with a boatload of camping gear and an additional passenger. Ahem, the gear is by far the heaviest part of the load. Though this is not Pierce's first rodeo, for this episode he's playing the part of the clown, a role usually reserved for the Rube.

The notorious Mister Gusty picks this afternoon to throw a tantrum. No sooner than they head out from the marina, Pierce is facing another gale force headwind, this time from the east. For Pete's sake, it's déjà vu all over again. He must also battle a mysterious whirlpool that will not permit his kayak to cross the center channel to the east side of the river where the beach is. After an exhausting three-and-a-half-hour effort, there's still no sign of the beach. Darkness is falling when Pierce decides to turn back. They'll return to the marina, hop in the car, and call it a night. Lesson learned.

After another hour of bone-chilling paddling in the dark, the marina is nowhere in sight. Pierce is now worried about hypothermia, so he decides to go ashore and set up camp. No problem. Isn't this fun, honey? This is classic Rube material.

When Pierce tries to step out of the boat, his legs are asleep and they buckle under him like a flimsy folding chair. He falls backward and goes under. Then he flounders face first, scraping his leg bloody on the rocky shore. After a pitch black, ankle-tweaking, knee-wrenching slog in waist-deep 45-degree water, Mae makes it safely to dry ground. Pierce must now secure the kayak so the current doesn't carry it away. Tussling in the dark with the thorny scrub, he tips the boat and douses the gear in the river. Pierce takes most of the lashing himself.

The entire shoreline is littered with sharp rocks, pointy scrub, and cactus. After raising the soggy tent, a scratched, bruised, and buck-naked Pierce hangs his bloody clothes in the desert shrub. He dances a careful two-step with the bush so he doesn't hang something else on a pointy object. If it weren't dark, it would have been quite a sight.

Hours of shivering inside a cold, damp tent on a hard bed of prickers makes the whole experience complete. Mae is worried that the bloody clothes will attract wild beasts, so she's awake all night thinking she hears rustling outside the tent. Pierce and Mae are party animals, but this is over the top.

In the morning light, the blood-smeared tent looks like a crime scene, so Pierce breaks camp helter-skelter before any other charges can be pinned on him. When they get home, he performs a ritual burning of the tent to destroy any evidence. Except the memories.

I'm sure this is precisely the type of togetherness Mae was hoping for. A romantic night together on the beach. The crackling of a campfire. The gentle riffle of the water. A bottle of wine. Reenacting the landmark surf scene in *From Here to Eternity*. I don't think she's in a hurry to try a Boys' Trip again. The boys can have this stuff. They deserve it.

Any doubts about the rigor or the physical demands of this annual challenge have been put to rest for good. The girls now know for sure that these things are not beer drinking boondoggles. They're tests of manliness and endurance designed to make men out of boys and sometimes succeeding. Overcoming a little hardship is a time-tested method of building heroic character in men. Making us into men more capable of protecting our families when the big bad wolf comes calling for real.

INTERLUDE: TRADITION! TRADITION!

Pierce's ordeal on the river in no way suggests that a guy can't go with a girl on an adventure trip and have a great experience. Some women are far better adventurers than many guys, the Rube included. But a girl deserves a trip of her own, not a recycled Boys' Trip. She is her own unique source of wisdom, so a woman doesn't need a wilderness trip of any type. A woman seems able to summon the seasons at will. It's not called Father Nature.

A guy can learn something worthwhile from a good time no matter who he's with. When a trip goes really well, he might be moved to gratitude and praise, and those are fine habits to form. But lessons learned and wisdom gained from hardship tend to be more long-lasting and often life-changing. Even when everything goes awry, an adventure trip is still a success if a man's soul is awakened and stirred. Trials make us more aware of our weaknesses and our spiritual needs. Under stress, bad habits and sinful tendencies become more evident, and recognizing them makes us better prepared to curb them.

Our spiritual survival skills grow from our experience, but not solely by our own power. In matters of the soul, every man needs capable spiritual mentors. Teachers who help keep us away from trouble. The Holy Bible and the teachings of the Church are our essential guides, our maps to holiness. In Pierce's case it was innocence, but when the Rube goes against tradition he's armed primarily with his own arrogance. Absent the Church's wisdom, a man is fighting the headwinds of the world without a chart or a moral compass. Separated from a group of like-minded pals, he's paddling alone against the culture's powerful, secular current.

A storehouse of essential supernatural survival skills is the fruit of the Church's Tradition. They can be ours if we humbly ask, seek, and knock.

RISK AND RETURN

"Who are the new folks?" I whisper as I nudge my pal Milo.

We're both sitting on the floor against the back wall of the chapel. Even though there are plenty of open chairs, Milo likes to keep stuff in front of him. It may be a technique he learned from his wrestling days. He doesn't want to be taken down by a surprise move from behind. As for me, I'm down here to evade the penetrating gaze of the group leader, an esteemed woman of God who answers to Saint Martha. The better to make mischief. It's a throwback to my grade school days. Makes me feel like a kid again.

Martha and her husband, Mack, plus Milo and a few others began this healing prayer group at the parish when a friend was diagnosed with aggressive melanoma. The cancer had already spread throughout his body, and his prognosis was very bad. His doctors gave him, at best, six months to live. Fifteen years later, he's an active middle school educator, still inspiring young people to pursue excellence. And the healing prayer group is still praying. The group hasn't missed a single Friday in fifteen years. Every week the same small core faithfully keeps it going. Once in a while, a new person or two shows up, usually to pray for a specific intention. Then they're gone.

The older couple up in the second row has been back now for three weeks.

Milo puts his finger to his lips, "Shhhh. I don't know," he whispers, "but they must have something big."

Since they've been here three straight Fridays, Milo thinks there must be something more serious than the everyday, garden-variety illness or pending surgery. People stop in to pray in a crisis, and once it's settled, we never see them again.

Milo understands human nature, but unlike the rest of us, he's honest and transparent about it. Too many of us treat God like a fairy godmother. We pray for stuff when we're desperate and don't think much about him any other time. Milo couldn't be mean if he tried, but he can be brutally frank. He won't cut you with sharp, but he'll bruise you with blunt. If you're offended by something Milo says about you, chances are it's because truth hurts.

Of course, I have a few personality quirks of my own. When I meet a new person, I have a habit that Vickie finds appalling. For fun, I will greet the new guy with dry humor or a wise crack, just to see how he takes it. Consequently, I risk offending a sensitive person straight away. I think I have no malicious intent, but the Rube's ways are a puzzle. I seem to embrace risk in other areas too, so hopefully this is only a harmless rhetorical adventure.

I figure it's a good icebreaker. If a person is easygoing, he won't be offended by the comment, and if he has a wry sense of humor, the remark might put him at ease right away. If he's tightly wound and takes offense, I apologize immediately and ask for his forgiveness. I could stand to repent more regularly, so this is good practice for me.

Milo seems to enjoy this conversational technique, and sometimes we practice it as a team. Vickie just can't abide this conduct and chides me frequently, "If you hope to have any friends at all, you can't do that."

I try to control myself more when she's around. However, Milo has a way of bringing out the worst in me.

The new couple, Ray and his wife, Grace, are both reserved and soft-spoken. Over time, we manage to learn more about them in short, cordial chats with Ray outside the chapel. They recently moved from New Orleans and don't know a soul in Arizona, except their son, who lives here and works in real estate.

The next week, the Rube figures he's had about enough of the idle chitchat. It's time to see if Ray is ready to crack the boy's inner circle.

Outside after praying the Rosary, Milo is standing with Ray, who's wearing a Hawaiian luau shirt with a loud floral design. I grab Ray by the arm, and exclaim, "Holy gumbo, Ray, who dressed you today? If you tossed your crawdad jambalaya on the front of that shirt nobody would notice."

Ray doesn't even blink. He fires back a pretty good zinger. "Who let you out in public? Is it Mardi Gras? With that big head of yours, you're a parade float all by yourself."

Milo howls. I mock wince and slap Ray on the back. "Good one, Ray. Round one goes to you."

This verbal sparring between guys harkens back to our childhood baseball days playing pepper or fungo. You learn to think quick or you paid a price. Even if a kid were in the proper fielding position, the odds are he'd take a hot grounder to a sensitive area sooner or later. You learned to always have your cup on you, and I don't mean in your bag back in the dugout. Milo and I liked Ray right off the bat.

We're surprised to learn that Ray is eighty years old. He moves deliberately and speaks really slowly, but he looks nowhere near eighty. His face is smooth and well preserved for a man his age, and his hair is full and well groomed, like he could be a television preacher on Sunday morning cable. Real distinguished.

There is something about the way he speaks softly, in that soothing N'awlins drawl, that says this man has seen a lot of things in his life, and there's some deep wisdom there. His vaguely wistful tone hints that a lot of water has passed under his bridge, some of it maybe not so clean and pure. Not that much different from the rest of us.

Ray tells us that Grace has suffered from cancer before, but it has been in remission for a few years. They are old-school Catholics, and praying the Rosary is a fond tradition for them. They pray in thanksgiving for Grace's continued recovery. They are really glad to have found our little prayer group and are making our church their new parish.

It's only a few Fridays later when Ray comes to prayer group alone. The usual gleam in his eyes is gone. Grace's cancer has returned with a new intensity, and she isn't well enough to leave the house. Over the next few weeks, her condition worsens, and together with her doctors, she and Ray decide they aren't going to fight the cancer this time. They're just going to treat her pain.

Later, when Grace is admitted to hospice, Ray tells us he won't be joining us anymore. He'll be staying with Grace at the hospice home. Even though she has around-the-clock nursing care, Ray isn't going to leave her side.

Milo and I start visiting the hospice home at night to sit with Ray, bring him something to eat, and keep him company. Grace sleeps, while in the dimly lit corner of the room, Ray sits slowly rocking in the upholstered chair. With a calm, quiet voice, tinged ever so slightly with regret, he begins to tell us how he and Grace came to leave the bayou for the desert.

They had lived in New Orleans for decades, and enjoyed the charms the city is famous for. In Ray's case, I get the feeling he may have imbibed in his share of the wild stuff, maybe even caroused a bit with some of the shady characters in those parts. They had even become accustomed to the frequent hurricanes, if such a thing is possible. Ray had learned to take the advance weather warnings with a pinch of salt. The storm was never as bad as the forecast.

When the advance evacuation warnings started coming through for the latest storm, Ray figured this one was no worse than all the others. He and Grace would button the place up, stay home, and ride out the storm.

Strong winds and severe rain quickly knocked out all the power and phone service. But they'd seen that before. Service would be back soon. Then the levees broke, releasing an unprecedented tidal wave that swamped every escape route. When the rain kept coming, Ray and many others realized too late that this storm was different.

Ray stops rocking and leans forward. His eyes well with tears, and his voice breaks as he looks skyward. "I made a terrible mistake. Lord, forgive me." He swallows hard. "Katrina . . ." Ray can't finish his thought, but he doesn't have to.

Milo and I sit spellbound as Ray weaves his account, his voice barely above a whisper.

With no chance of escape they hunker down inside the house. When the massive wall of water and debris strikes, the doors and windows present little resistance. Murky water rushes in through every crack, and creeps quickly up the walls inside the house. Desperate, Ray lifts the heavy wood dining chairs up on the dining table. They clamber up on the chairs to keep their heads above the rising froth.

The water is scarcely two feet from the ceiling when Ray makes a gutsy call. He gathers his remaining strength, grabs Grace by the arm, and plunges beneath the turbid water. He thrashes blindly to an opening where a window has been swept away. He struggles through, pulling Grace with him. After what feels like an eternity, their breath gone and Ray's strength flagging, they burst to the surface outside the house.

He's clinging desperately to Grace in the swirling torrent just below roof level. Ray pulls her over to the roof and grasps the eave with his free hand. With a strength not his own, he boosts Grace up to the eave and then onto the roof. He pulls himself up after her, and they scoot shakily up to the peak.

Clinging tight to each other, they watch the floodwaters lap row after row of shingles, drawing ever closer to the ridge-line.

The rain continued but the floodwaters subside mere inches from the peak.

"Watch and pray," Ray whispers. "I found my faith again that day. We needed a miracle, and the Lord was there for us." In Ray's mind, there's no doubt it was the hand of God.

Ray and Grace endure a long, cold night, huddled on the roof. Shivering and praying, holding tight to the only thing they have left. By morning, the storm passed, the rain tapered off and a rescue crew was able to reach them.

Ray and Grace's ordeal would be a critical test for young people in peak physical condition. For a couple in their seventies, their survival seems more like a supernatural intervention because of one minor detail I haven't mentioned. Something that makes Ray's tale even more outrageous, nearly preposterous.

Neither Grace nor Ray could swim a lick.

When their lives were on the line, Ray did something he'd never done in his life. How does a guy who sinks like a stone swim like Ray did that day?

Grace and Ray survived, but their hardships were far from over. They lost everything they owned. Flood insurance premiums in Louisiana were exorbitant, so, like many folks, they had gone without it. Ray took a calculated risk and lost. If that weren't bad enough, Ray had entrusted his retirement savings to his son, who invested it in what seemed like safe real estate deals. Just a short time after Katrina, the Great Recession hit, and real estate markets collapsed nationwide. In a heartbeat, Ray's life savings had evaporated.

Once a wealthy and successful man, Ray is now eighty years old and flat broke. For the first time since childhood, he's dependent on someone else.

Ray's mind is a thousand miles away. He sighs, "I had a lot of dreams about what I would do with my life, but I never dreamed I would be doing this."

He clasps his hands and gives Milo and I a wry smile. "But it's OK. The Lord has been good to me."

Through it all, Ray is at peace. His tone is one of quiet determination, not resignation, and his voice has not a hint of bitterness. A world where everybody is a victim would expect him to be filled with resentment, grumbling about bad luck, forsaking God, or looking for someone to blame. Instead Ray comes to prayer group to pray for others. People facing real hardship.

Grace's cancer does not retreat into remission this time. At the end, Ray stayed awake night and day with her, not even leaving her bedside to shower or freshen up. If she awoke, he wanted to be there to reassure and comfort her. He had saved her once before, and he was not about to leave her alone at the threshold of eternity.

Ray no longer has a small fortune to spend in a comfortable, carefree retirement. When his time comes, he won't have much to bequeath to his posterity. But he'll leave something more valuable than a mountain of stuff. He'll pass on the legacy of a faithful, humble man with a courageous spirit. A guy who persevered through many hardships, which didn't bring him to ruin but refined his character. Even if he ends his life destitute in the world's eyes, Ray will be remembered for courageous gifts more excellent than any material things: forgiveness to his son, undying love for his wife, and devotion to his faith.

The culture fills our heads with garbage about what a real man is and what a hero looks like. Much of what the world is selling goes against what we know to be true about beauty, goodness, and heroic virtue. But too often we buy into it anyway.

A guy like Ray is an unlikely candidate for the role of a Hollywood superhero. But the story of this modest, soft-spoken, gentle Cajun contains more truth about authentic manhood and genuine heroism than a galaxy of bogus superhero comics or movies. Yeah, Ray seems like a typical average old guy. But in the real world, Ray is a true action hero.

INTERLUDE: KING ME

The existence of evil pretty much guarantees that a guy is going to face hardship and loss. Adversity tests the mettle of even the fittest of men and the holiest of souls. No man escapes untried. Where does he turn, and to whom does he look when he's faced with physical danger, open hostility, persecution, or suffering?

Much of the country is steeped in a culture war, where a guy with traditional values and morals may feel like he's behind enemy lines. So, if you're uneasy sometimes, there's nothing wrong with you. It's not a bad thing to be restless.

There is strength in numbers, so for encouragement and support a guy could look to everyday heroes like Ray. These are guys who can take a hit and pull themselves to their feet. Men who don't run from trouble, and don't back down from a fight. Guys who don't live to feed their appetites and indulge their fantasies, but look to serve, comfort, and inspire others. But these men don't seek publicity. Their humility won't abide with hypocrisy. To find them a guy has to go looking for them. You almost have to be one.

If we're honest, we'll admit that men don't do well for very long when we're content. Otherwise Adam might still be in Eden. Being satisfied doesn't seem to bring out the best in us. We quickly get too comfortable for our own good. I'm thinking of a bloated King Henry VIII lounging at table with a meaty drumstick in one fist and wine goblet in the other, ample belly lapping over his sash, greasy morsels staining his waistcoat. This is a guy who began his reign athletic, lean, hungry, and noble.

The Rube has a final note of optimism for you: It's actually a blessing to be living during times of challenge. Some of our best work comes when we're unsettled. This is our shot to trade out video game heroics for real-world virtue.

WHO ARE YOU?

From the beginning, the creature known as man has been a tough sell. Accepting his Creator's word at face value wasn't good enough for him. It wasn't enough for man to be like God. Man wanted to be God. Even an all-powerful Creator couldn't persuade the skeptical creature to whom he had given a free will. From the moment he started listening to outside voices, man has suffered an identity crisis.

From his first fateful decision, the free man has had to discern between real things and counterfeits, between truth and lies. Stuff that looked like fruit, smelled and felt like fruit, sometimes wasn't at all good for him. And his choices are not getting easier.

Now a guy must choose even the type of man he will be. The world proposes many versions of the ideal man through a relentless torrent of information, entertainment, and advertising. Social media presents a whole new and powerful source of pressure and distortion about manhood.

There are many subgroups and variations, but by the Rube's reckoning, the world proposes two main identity choices for men today, the Interesting Man (IM) and the Typical Average

Guy (TAG). But beware, these labels are deceptive, devious, and self-serving. Everybody has something to sell.

The IM is the king of his man-made world. He is defined by his stuff. He never stops acquiring, stockpiling, consuming, and using. Always more and better. His life is, at its core, a contest to continually prove himself. A quest to remain relevant and interesting in the eyes of the world. Of course, the ultimate IM is that masterful marketing creation, "The Most Interesting Man in the World" (MIM).

Recently I walked into a restaurant in the mountain town of Williams, Arizona, and I couldn't believe my good fortune. With all the exotic places in the entire world at his whim, the MIM was right there in the bar. True to his image, he was surrounded by a gaggle of women. He's much shorter in person. That's encouraging since guys always compare ourselves against other guys, especially celebrities. I feel more interesting already.

From across the room, the MIM and his group appeared lively and attractive, but when I got close enough to kick his tires, I found that the entire entourage was pretty flat. Sadly, they were also stiff, one-dimensional, and very poor conversationalists. Not all that interesting. Too bad, there was so much I wanted to ask him. Staring into his vacant cardboard eyes I can only imagine I hear his cardboard tongue preaching his trademark message, "Stay thirsty, my friends."

His slogan is optimistic and amusing if interpreted as the ambitious man's continuous search for truth and significance. But what if his advice is translated into the cynical language of the consumer culture? Could it be a little darker? His advice could as easily be, "Never stop acquiring, consuming, and using. You can have it all."

Don't misunderstand. I love the MIM. He is pure marketing brilliance. But the fat lady will sing for him the same as us. And when she does, he better be in hot pursuit of ultimate Truth instead of his next big thrill. I have a hunch that If he's not, he could end up like the guy in scripture who gains the whole world but forfeits his soul (cf. Mk 8:36). Being thirsty will be the least of his worries.

Odds are you are what the world would call a typical average guy (TAG). You're not a secret agent, professional athlete, movie star, or fashion mogul. You don't park your private jet on your own island. You don't spend $395 for the latest "designer tailored joggers." Those things are reserved for the IM. Dude, they're sweat pants.

The TAG has mundane, real-world commitments like a job, a wife, kids, relatives, in-laws, responsibilities, and a mortgage. He lives with inconvenient things like boundaries and limits. TAGs cut grass, fill cavities, and pound nails. They're bean counters, bug killers, appraisers, and unemployed, unpublished authors. The TAG is the target of relentless marketers selling all the stuff that will elevate him to the status of an IM.

If you're feeling depressed about now, no worries. The Rube has some more back-of-the-envelope anthropology for you; the IM and the TAG don't exist in reality. They are stereotypes; straw men created by the marketing gurus of pop culture. They are perpetual fuel for the consumer merry-go-round. Genius.

The Rube herewith proposes a countercultural alternative, the True Man. Every man, at his core, has the seed of True Manship. He is a True Man in the making. We are formed from the same clay, breathed with the same spirit, our souls encased in the same flesh and bone. Every man has as much potential for quit as grit, vice as virtue, cowardice as heroism. A guy can as soon be Doctor Jekyll as Mister Hyde or anywhere from a great saint to a big sinner. The difference between the True Man and the rest, then, is the degree to which the man knows what is true, seeks what is good, and does what is right.

The journey to True Manship is a lifelong mission to uncover the answers to life's big questions. You might think you've got everything under control. You may not be searching for anything in particular. You might think you have all the answers you need. But even when you're at the top of your game, it's good to step back and consider a new or different idea. It's how you stay at the top.

The Rube's challenge is to rethink your life from a new angle. Dig up something you buried awhile back, or dust off something long forgotten or dismissed. Reconnect with an old friend. Check for yourself things others have abandoned or declared fruitless. Gain a new perspective.

A guy needs to follow his heart where his honest inquiries lead, even when they take him to unpopular or dangerous places, or into situations that risk his image, his popularity, or his career. That will require courage.

Adventure is essential to every man's quest for truth, and the wilderness is the great equalizer. On the trail, the status and trappings of the man-made world fall away. A guy has no title, no limo driver, and no executive secretary to carry his man stuff up the hill. He doesn't need those things out here, and they don't make a guy a better man anyway. They're called trappings. No wonder.

In nature, the truth about manhood can come into focus when the clutter of the material world is left behind. A guy needs to go there regularly to think about invisible things, preferably with another guy or two. A life of heroism, integrity, and truth is every man's destiny. The Boys' Trip is an entry level ticket to that adventure—the adventure of True Manship.

TRUE MANSHIP

Conditioning and endurance help a man run the race and stay the course. But does a physical challenge prepare him for the rigors of the spiritual life? Does doing hard things in the natural world accelerate his journey to True Manship?

If you give a whole blood donation every eight weeks for a year, the blood service provider gives you a custom calendar and a greeting card proclaiming you a "blood hero." A whole blood donation takes about twenty minutes. Chad has donated platelets every four weeks for more than forty years. This is the big kahuna of lifesaving donations, requiring two to three hours of needle time and the rest of the day for recovery. If a whole blood donor is a hero, then what does that make Chad? How many lives have been saved by his quiet, heroic sacrifice? A guy would do well to get some of Chad's platelets. It's superhero blood.

Capp's marriage was broken by his wife's drug addiction, leaving him a single parent of their two kids. Then he suffered a layoff from his professional job and faced looming financial devastation. A lesser man might become bitter and broken. Capp responds by accepting a humble position, well below his qualifications, in order to meet his responsibilities. He steadily rebuilds his life and career while raising his kids to become strong, productive young adults. He shows them how a man makes his way honorably through choppy waters.

Walter hiked much more when he was younger, before the toll of five knee surgeries. He's a physician with a wife, five kids, and a crazy schedule. Time off is scarce, but he takes his older kids to Washington D.C. for the March for Life. Instead of a winter beach vacation, they march for miles through the worst blizzard in a decade. Once in a while, a guy can make a bold statement with a richly symbolic action. The bigger witness is the quiet heroism Walter displays every day as the physical and spiritual provider and protector for his family. Real-life action heroes put others before themselves.

Milo has prayed the Rosary every day for more than fifteen years; over 5,500 days and counting. This traditional devotion requires daily sacrifice and concentrated effort. He doesn't do it for himself, he's appealing for heavenly help for other people. Doubtless, many intentions have been granted and prayers answered on behalf of this extraordinarily devoted friend. A guy would be blessed to be included in the Gnome's prayer intentions.

These are guys who appear to the world to be nothing special. What they have in common is time invested out in nature, away from the corrosive consumer environment. When a guy gets out of the noise, peace can enter. He has a chance to consider things invisible.

What makes a guy a True Man has nothing to do with the stuff he has acquired. It has everything to do with the virtue he's gained. But the True Man is never finished. He is a work in progress until the end, and he advances by making an ever-greater gift of himself to others.

As long as we can become greater souls, the Boys' Trip will go on, *Deo volente*. In our senior years, our High Middle Ages, our activities might need to be scaled back a tad. Our shot at free-climbing El Capitan is probably past, but we won't waste a trip binge-watching fantasy sports.

My pal Andre uses a powerchair, but that doesn't stop him from four-wheeling off-road. He ventures by Jeep into the remote wilderness with his son for several days at a stretch. He's showing us whippersnappers how a True Man overcomes challenges and lives with humility, grace, and joy to the final buzzer. Andre will be 83 years of age in a few days.

But the path will not get smoother or easier. The lure of the world is strong. Our passion for seeking truth must be stronger.

Pontius Pilate was the prefect of the Roman province of Judea at the time of Jesus. He was among the most powerful, influential men of the age. In his domain, he wielded the authority of Caesar, the emperor-god of the vast Roman Empire. The intoxicating power over life and death was at his command.

Pilate had the awesome responsibility of interrogating and evaluating Jesus in person. In the end, Pilate's legacy consists of three words he left hanging in midair as he sent Jesus to the cross.

They are the same words that should challenge every man to his core. A question that haunts the souls of men two millennia later. Words that inspire legions of True Men to lives of heroic virtue.

"Pilate said to him, 'What is truth?'" (Jn 18:38)

No less than Pilate, each of us has the same crucial decision to make.

What will be the fate of the God-man, Jesus of Nazareth?

Do I let Him die?

Or do I allow the Truth to set me free?

ABOUT THE AUTHOR

Brian Weber is a Cold War veteran who served as the captain of a nuclear missile combat crew. After protecting the free world from nuclear destruction, he has since been occupied as an entrepreneur, a small business owner, and a freelance writer. He facilitates men's faith study groups, and has been leading men on outdoor excursions since 2001. Weber is a graduate of the U.S. Air Force Academy, and he earned his MBA from the University of Arizona. He lives in Phoenix, Arizona, with his wife. They have three adult children and seven grandchildren. In real life, he is usually not serious for this long. Time's up.

Contact the author at www.TrueManship.com